IRISH WATERSIDE WALKS

IRISH WATERSIDE WALKS

Michael Fewer

PASSPORT BOOKS
NTC/Contemporary Publishing Group

This edition published in 1999 by Passport Books
A division of NTC/Contemporary Publishing Group, Inc.
4255 West Touhy Avenue, Lincolnwood (Chicago), IL 60646-1975, U.S.A.

© Michael Fewer 1997
Maps and illustrations by Michael Fewer

Published in conjunction with
Gill & Macmillan Ltd
Goldenbridge
Dublin 8

Design and print origination by O'K Graphic Design, Dublin

Printed by ColourBooks Ltd, Dublin

This book is typeset in 9½/12 point Cochin.

International Standard Book Number: 0-8442-2389-1
Library of Congress Catalog Card Number: 98-68300

I dedicate this book to my mother, Mary Fewer, a woman of great character who enriched the lives of everyone she came in contact with; she passed away quietly in February 1996.

CONTENTS

INTRODUCTION

In ancient Ireland, springs, rivers and lakes, having their origin in the underworld, were thought to be magic; in the year I spent researching and preparing this guide I came across many of the places that must have inspired this awe, and found it difficult not to be so affected myself.

Water enlivens and adorns our landscapes in a unique way, whether it be through a glass-like lake on those rare, still days, mistily duplicating the beauty of the world around, or the constant, lively movement and susurrescence of a mountain brook. Due to the nature of the geology and climate of Ireland, we are blessed with the fact that there are few places in the land far from a lake or water course. There was a time when the importance of these water courses for travel, water supply, fishing and the provision of power for manufacturing was considerable, but today, with the exception of the great rivers such as the Shannon or Barrow, the active use of the many hundreds of Ireland's smaller water courses is confined to a few dedicated anglers, and their waters and banks have receded, overgrown, almost forgotten, into the landscape. For walkers these erstwhile backwaters provide a contrasting alternative to the mountain wilderness, with the advantage, that some will find welcome, of not requiring any strenuous climbing.

In the preparation and research of this book I spent an enjoyable year seeking out a collection of these hidden places to lay before you, in addition to including better known places such as the Clare Glens in Tipperary and the Lakes of Killarney which have long been noted for their particular beauty and have attracted visitors since tourism was in its infancy.

My search for suitable walks was not without frustrating setbacks, such as driving halfway across Ireland and setting out merrily on walks that came to a full stop after a few minutes; in some cases I found great walks but, due to the roughness of the terrain or doubts regarding access, I have reluctantly had to exclude these from this publication. I realise, however, I have only scratched the surface, and would be most interested to hear from readers of great walks I missed.

Most of my walking was done in summertime, because that is when growth is heaviest; there is little point recommending a walk that is passable in winter but an impenetrable jungle of nettles and brambles in summer, and believe me, I came across many of these.

Rivers, canals and lakes provide a unique habitat for flora and fauna due to the physical conditions they promote on the adjacent shores and the fact that, except for the odd town or village, our watersides are relatively undeveloped and undisturbed by man. Walking in these places will bring you into contact with a range of species that are not so common elsewhere.

The willow tree is rarely seen at its full and wonderful mature growth elsewhere, and indeed, one of the only places you will see the characteristic rugged bark of an old alder that has achieved perfection is on a riverbank. A unique and special series of plants and flowers are only to be seen beside water. On these walks you will become familiar with the great golden cups of marsh marigolds; you may be surprised to find that a variety of forget-me-not loves and thrives in damp places, and you may find yourself marvelling at the variety of grasses and reeds that flourish at the margins of lakes and rivers. In summertime a tall and colourful balsam, said to have come to Ireland as seeds hidden in jute sacks from the Far East, can be enjoyed, sometimes extending for miles, along our big rivers.

Bird-watchers will find that the majestic heron is the king of our rivers and canals, and reigns over a population that includes the shy waterhen, the bobbing dipper and the swift kingfisher, all of them surprisingly common away from 'civilisation'. Swans can be seen everywhere, and mallards are common, but the great-crested grebe is perhaps a little rarer, as is the cormorant, a bird that is normally seen along our coasts but can surprise you by his appearance on water as far from the sea as you can go in Ireland.

Animals likely to be seen close to our waterways include the stoat, the mink and the otter. The stoat, that little wiry and blood-thirsty carnivore, is more common in the west of the country, while the mink, all survivors of escapees from mink farms, have found a niche in every part of Ireland. I was delighted during my research to see many more otters than stoats or mink; the otter has not suffered the same decline in Ireland as it has over the rest of Europe, and signs of the animal have even recently been found in the heart of Dublin under O'Connell Bridge. I had a number of encounters with the beautiful creature during my walks; perhaps the closest took place early one morning on the Gweebarra river in Donegal, an experience I will not forget. Remember, early morning and late evening are always the best times to see the wildlife of waterways; and the waters themselves are often at their most picturesque at these times also.

SOME POINTERS AND ADVICE
Take care! Water may be beautiful to look at, but it can drown you! Be careful close to deep water, particularly if you are on your own; a simple

trip over a bramble at the water's edge can leave you, at best, cold and wet and feeling very foolish. Taking a break sitting on a riverbank or footbridge is enjoyable, but be careful with cameras and other valuables; archaeologists with scuba gear have done very well out of the legions of people who have dropped things where they cannot be retrieved.

Be careful leaving the car in isolated places especially near bigger cities, and make sure you leave no valuables in sight in the car.

MAPS

As most of these walks follow physical features that, outside of an earthquake or two, are unlikely to alter too much in the foreseeable future, the sketch maps accompanying each walk description should suffice for basic information. It is always worthwhile, however, and adds to the value of your excursion, to carry an up-to-date OS map. This will give you lots of additional and useful information on features of the countryside near by, and will help you to enjoy the overall experience all the more. Maps mentioned in the text are the most up to date available at time of writing.

WALKING TIMES

The times noted are what I suggest it should take an average walker to complete the walk; breaks for snacks or further exploration or rests are not included in these times. They are based on my own experience of the terrain as I found it when I walked there. If you are walking for pleasure rather than simply for exercise, I would expect you would add at least an additional three-quarters of an hour to every 2 hours walking, just for stopping, exploring and generally assimilating your surroundings. These walks are suggested, not for their potential for providing exercise alone, but for the more holistic pleasures of leisure and relaxation.

Of necessity, many of these walks involve 'there-and-back' routes rather than loops. While I am always interested in returning a different way, I have to say that on the return there are new angles and aspects and details unseen on the outward journey; the change in the light of the day alone can create a different scene.

RIGHTS-OF-WAY

Many of these routes follow riverside paths through privately owned agricultural land. I have not included any routes where trespass was expressly forbidden, but times and circumstances and owners change, so be vigilant for such notices at all times; if in doubt, ask at the nearest farm. Please respect the places you pass through and the crops planted. If you come across livestock, do not disturb them. Take particular care in fields with cattle, especially if there are calves present, and do not enter fields where there may be a bull!

─── ACKNOWLEDGMENTS ───

My thanks to the many who encouraged and assisted me during my travels around Ireland seeking out waterside walks, in particular Alastair, Daphne, Carrie and Emily Begg in Antrim, Michael and Mary Swanton in Letterkenny, Suzanne Clarke in Carlow, Derry and Bernadette Solan in Mullingar, John Holmes in Kilkenny, Oliver Hawes in Cobh, Jim and Ann O'Callaghan, and James, Marjorie and Emma Doran in Dublin. A special thanks is due to David Herman for his very practical help. Eveleen Coyle deserves my gratitude for coming up with the idea for this book, an idea that introduced me to more of the seemingly endless beautiful corners of the Irish countryside.

Finally, my thanks to my family whose support and tolerance are much appreciated, and to Teresa, as always, for the company and the fun!

AUTHOR'S NOTE

The author and publishers have taken every care to ensure that the information contained in this book is accurate at the time of writing. In the nature of the subject, however, changes can and do occur in the countryside. Some of the walks are over lands and river banks where walkers are not currently forbidden. However, owners and attitudes can change, so if in any doubt ask permission. The author and publishers shall have no liability in respect of any loss or damage, however caused, arising out of the use of this guide.

MAP OF WALK LOCATIONS

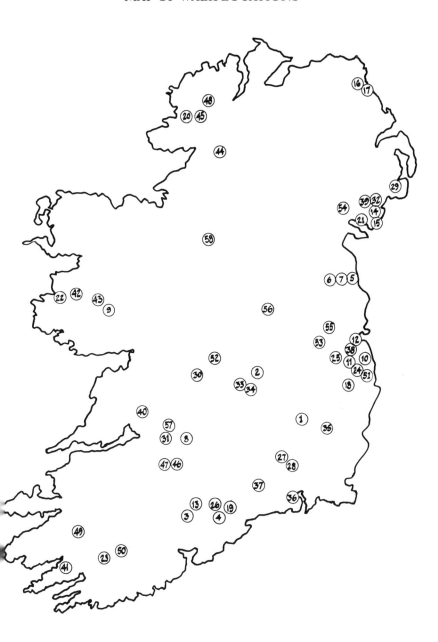

Key to Maps

River or canal

Lake or Reservoir

Road

Main Route N14

Track or path

Castle

Parking Ⓟ

Return point

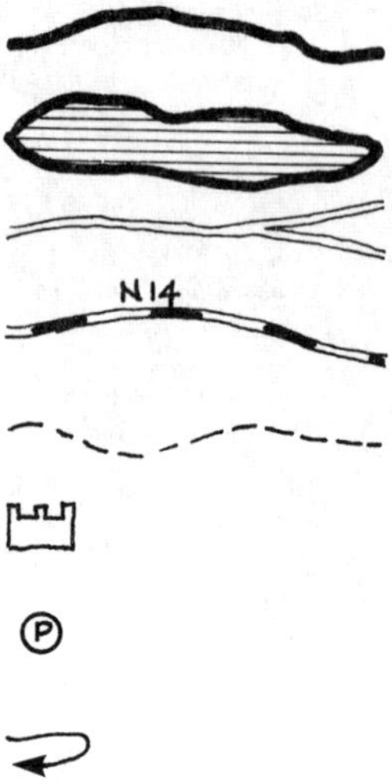

RIVERS

THE BARROW RIVER

The Barrow River is Ireland's second longest river after the Shannon, and drains a large portion of the south-east of the country during its course between the Slieve Bloom Mountains and Waterford Harbour where, combined with the Nore and the Suir, it reaches the sea. In medieval times it was an important trading route linking the midlands to the sea, and in the late 18th century a canal link was constructed connecting the Barrow with the Grand Canal system, thus making it possible to ship goods between the major cities of Dublin, Limerick and Waterford. The continued existence of the navigation with its towpaths makes the Barrow a wonderful river-walking route, and the frequent villages and towns along its banks make it possible to walk almost the whole length of the river in relatively easy stages. An example of such stages would be:

Monasterevin to Vicarstown:	3 hours
Vicarstown to Athy:	2½ hours
Athy to Carlow:	5¼ hours
Carlow to Leighlinbridge:	2¾ hours
Leighlinbridge to Mhuine Bheag:	1¼ hours
Mhuine Bheag to Borris:	4¾ hours
Borris to Graiguenamanagh:	3 hours
Graiguenamanagh to St Mullins:	1¾ hours

The towpaths vary from well-maintained grass lawns to somewhat overgrown paths and even stretches of tarmac.

All of the stages listed above have their own particular character related to the local geology, agriculture and history; I have selected the Carlow to Leighlinbridge stretch as an example of what one can expect.

♦ WALK 1: THE BARROW RIVER: FROM CARLOW TOWN TO LEIGHLINBRIDGE,
CO. CARLOW ♦

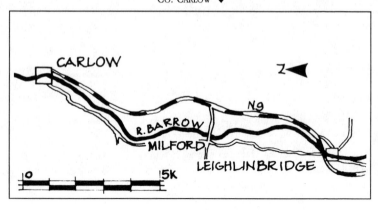

Walking time: 2¾ hours
Terrain: Grassy towpaths, sometimes a little overgrown; it is useful to have a walking stick to use as a machete if nettle growth is high.
How to get there: Carlow is on the N9, 83 km south of Dublin.
Map: OS Half-inch Sheet 19

From Carlow town cross the bridge over the Barrow into Graiguecullen, and turn right past 19th-century mill buildings to follow the river south past Carlow lock. A marina has been recently constructed and the towpath past it renovated, so a good pace can be maintained for the beginning of this walk. The thick wall of willows on the far side of the river soon gives way to lawns that slope down to the water's edge from a series of houses in their own grounds; one of them is Otter Holt Riverside Lodge, a hostel which offers canoeing on the Barrow.

Ten minutes after leaving the town the Barrow has taken you out of County Carlow and into County Laois and the countryside, with the long, low Castlecomer Plateau stretching along the western horizon, a patchwork quilt of emerald green fields. Soon the river divides, the towpath following the navigable channel while the river proper passes to the far side of a long, narrow tree-covered island. At the riverside spears of purple loosestrife surrounded banks of Himalayan balsam that waved pendulous pink heads in the breeze when I passed. I was told by an elderly man at St Mullins that the balsam had come as seeds in woolsacks that had been made in China, and had been distributed along our rivers and canals by barges in the 19th century. Another exotic plant, the origins of which I wondered about, was the widespread bamboo I found along this section of the Barrow.

The fine cut-stone constructed Clogrennan lock terminates the narrow island, beside a picturesque lock cottage, and the river merges again. On the far side when I passed there were a few tall stands of giant hogweed, almost as tall as small trees. Not far from the lock is a house within a walled site, with small circular towers at each corner. Further on, across the road, a tall ivy-covered Gothic bawn gateway made from cut-limestone is all that remains of Clogrennan Castle, victim of sieges in the 16th and 17th centuries.

To the west is the gaunt ruin of a mansion built by the Rochfords in the late 18th century. For a change, this ruin is not the result of burning by Republican forces during the War of Independence, but of neglect and abandonment.

About here you pass back into County Carlow again; the river is now broad and slow flowing, and I was fortunate enough to see a kingfisher, darting past in a blur of electric blue. The river bends around to the left and enters a long straight tree-lined stretch with the pinnacled tower of Cloydagh church rising ahead. If you never considered willow trees to be beautiful, you may change your mind along this stretch; in their full maturity it is wonderful the way their grey-blue foliage reflects the light.

About 80 minutes after setting out, the towpath touches on the public road again as it approaches Milford, and the river divides again to serve the millrace. When I passed I enjoyed the sight of a large otter playing along the far side, and as I stopped to watch, so too did he, gazing curiously over at me until I made a move, reaching for my camera, whereupon he dived sinuously and swam for cover.

When the road bridge is met climb steps on to the road; the towpath beyond the bridge tends to be overgrown, and there is more to see from a short diversion on the road. The castellated Alexander's Mill comes into sight now on the far side of the river, very picturesque with a foreground of bridges and weirs. A hundred people were employed here in the 19th century at malting and corn milling. In 1891 Carlow was the first inland town in Ireland to have electric street lighting, and the power for that lighting was generated by an early hydroelectric turbine here in the mill at Milford. Continuing this tradition, a private turbine operates today to feed power into the national grid.

Continue past the many-arched bridge, the width of which indicates how the Barrow can flood in wintertime, and cross the canal by a lifting bridge to reach the towpath again. You are a little more than halfway to Leighlinbridge now, and this is a fine place to sit awhile, as I did, watching the pond skaters tracking along the glass-like surface of the water, and marvelling at the swallows coming straight at me, centimetres above the surface, only to swoop up and over the bridge before dropping down again on the other side.

This is a very peaceful stretch of river, the far side heavily wooded with oak, ash, and of course those great silvery crack willows. Over on the right, less than 1 km away, look out for a prominent wooded hillock called Bawnree Wood. There are ruins of a pre-penal church on the west side of the hill, and it is a strong local tradition that the defeated King James and a cavalry bodyguard camped overnight in the trees there on their way south after the Battle of the Boyne in 1690.

The trees close in on both sides now as the river divides again, and the towpath follows a rampart dividing the canal from a deep drainage ditch. Butterflies were abundant here when I passed, and I must have seen all the common Irish varieties within a few miles, including red admirals, peacocks, painted ladies and common blues. Electric blue and green damselflies were plentiful here also, and dragonflies like tiny model aircraft hummed by, hoovering up small insects.

As the towpath comes out into the open again, there is a brief glimpse of Mount Leinster on the horizon. The traffic on the main road is visible now 1 km away; take pity on all those poor travellers concentrating on speed and traffic. The flat meadows on the far side of the river usually flood in wintertime, attracting great flocks of curlews, lapwings and gulls, and creating a scene that resembles the plains of Africa.

The river bears around gently to the right and begins a long, straight, island-studded run towards Leighlinbridge, marked by a church tower on the horizon. The islands along here provide useful cover for mallards and you should also see herons about.

After the sadly ruined lock-keeper's cottage (under which the drainage ditch runs) the towpath passes under a well-designed modern bridge that carries the main road. Here the nettles and long grass are left behind; a well-kept lawn takes you the final few hundred metres into the pleasant village of Leighlinbridge, birthplace of John Tyndal, educationalist, scientist and mountaineer, and Cardinal Moran, Archbishop of Sydney.

♦ WALK 2: THE INFANT BARROW RIVER, CO. LAOIS ♦

This is a fine walk up into a most picturesque old red sandstone gorge through which the infant River Barrow cuts, a short distance from the place where it rises. It is a magical place of rocks and waterfalls; legend tells us that the spring from which the Barrow rises is enchanted, and if anyone were to disturb its waters, or even look upon it, the spring would disgorge a deluge of such magnitude that it would inundate all the land around the Slieve Blooms.

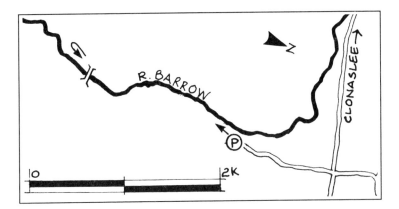

Walking time: 1 hour there and back
Terrain: Woodland paths, sometimes narrow and muddy, not suitable for young children.
How to get there: About 3.2 km east of Clonaslee take a right turn following a sign for Glenbarrow; a little over 3 km further on Glenbarrow car park is reached.
Map: OS Discovery Series Sheet 54

From the car park, go right, down a narrow boreen between stone walls bejewelled with bluebells, wild strawberries, stitchwort and ferns. Within a couple of minutes the Barrow can be heard rushing below; follow the path to the left, parallel with the river, through a coniferous wood carpeted with wood sorrel and violets.

At clearings between the trees it can be seen that the river runs through a deep, steep-sided ravine, having worn its way down through boulder clay and old red sandstone for eons. The far side of the ravine is hung down with gorse, hawthorn, rowan and birch; tree trunks and branches richly covered with a thick layer of velvet moss indicate how sheltered and humid the climate is here.

Fifteen minutes after starting out, the path emerges into a broad clearing. Here the Barrow broadens to pass over a series of flat pavements of bedrock formed many millions of years ago from river-borne detritus and sediments, the eroded remains of a great mountain range, now long disappeared. Rock was quarried from this place many years ago; careful examination will reveal holes drilled in places in the rock for the insertion of dynamite. Watch out for dippers and grey wagtails, which are common here.

The path ascends alongside the river, and 5 minutes later you will reach a marvellous cascade called the Clamphole. Search the flat, exposed pavements not far from the path to find fossil ripple marks, like those left behind on a sandy beach after the tide has gone out. These particular ripples were left in a similar way by an ancient river that flowed north an incredible 345 million years ago.

Climb up steeply towards the top of the waterfall to find the river pouring over two more, smaller, falls just above. Beyond, the noise of the cascades recedes as you ascend the path high above the river into the tree-tops. It levels out at canopy level, giving a bird's eye view of the tops of rowans, oaks, hazels, hawthorns and hollies. Beyond the tree-tops the heather of the open mountain can be seen. Compare the almost non-existence of undergrowth beneath the conifers up to the left with the rich and varied herbage under the deciduous trees on the right. Follow the path carefully downhill to reach a timber footbridge and cross the river; see how an oak tree on the far side has colonised a sandstone outcrop, exploiting any available cleavages and cracks for its roots.

Continue upstream along a narrow path; keep a look-out for holly trees beside the path which have had their bark eaten by wild goats. There are some potholes exposed in the rocks of the riverbed; these were formed over eons by falls of water that no longer exist. After a couple of minutes, just as the main path turns uphill, follow a faint path parallel to the river until stopped by a tributary coming from the right. This is the end of the walk; there is a grassy bank on which to sit and absorb the atmosphere of the place before returning by the same route.

THE RIVER BLACKWATER

The River Blackwater is one of Ireland's great rivers, rising in the mountains of Kerry and flowing eastwards as it drains upwards of 2,900 sq. km of the south of Ireland and after a course of 160 km enters the sea at Youghal. Most of its course is eastwards, but abruptly at Cappoquin it turns south for the sea. It is a grand, broad and slow-flowing river that, like the Shannon, Boyne, Barrow, Nore and Suir, gave early colonists and invaders access to the interior of the country, and like those rivers its banks are scattered with prosperous country towns, castles and great houses.

I describe two walks on the Blackwater, the first starting in the bustling County Cork town of Fermoy, and the second at the bridge of historic Lismore in County Waterford.

♦ WALK 3: THE RIVER BLACKWATER AT FERMOY, CO. CORK ♦

This walk, which introduces you to the grandeur of the Blackwater, is a long figure of eight loop (with a tail!) which takes you from the town upriver, back around through the outskirts of the town, then downstream along the riverbank before returning.

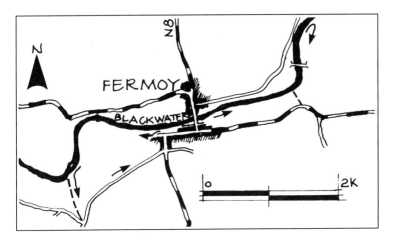

Walking time: 2 hours and 25 minutes
Terrain: Riverside paths, sometimes muddy and a little overgrown, and tarmac side roads.
How to get there: Fermoy is 51 km north of Cork on the N8.
Map: OS Half-inch Sheet 22

Leave the bridge at Fermoy and walk west along the south bank of the river past the Grand Hotel. Even here, 45 km from its outlet into the Atlantic, the Blackwater is a broad, strong-flowing river, darkly reflecting the tall trees lining its banks. To the left is a stone-walled demesne, where a bit further along you will find a holy well dedicated to St Bernard, which unfortunately looked anything but holy when I passed!

Shortly after, a stile is climbed and a grassy path is followed around a tributary thick with water lilies and reedmace to reach the riverbank again. Little timber platforms for anglers extend over the water's edge, fringed here with reeds and bunches of marsh forget-me-nots. Along here, where the waters darkly reflect the thickly wooded far bank, it is easy to see why the river was called the Blackwater or *Abhann Dubh*.

A series of stiles is crossed as, 20 minutes after setting out, the river bears around to the left and the anglers' path skirts fields where crops of barley and maize were growing when I passed. Soon the ground to the left rises, and the path follows the riverbank through bushes and outcrops of bedrock into a tall wood of spruce trees, from where there is a fine vista of the river as it broadens and sweeps majestically around towards the west.

The path leaves the river behind now and passes through a dark and green wood, taking the right turn at a fork. Fences line both sides of the path, creating a long narrow corridor to a tunnel under a bridge, by which the landowner presumably gains access to the other half of a garden. A tributary comes babbling down from the left, and the path follows it upstream, still between fences.

Fifteen minutes after entering the fenced corridor a fork is reached; take the left turn to reach the public road and turn left, turning left yet again at a junction, and follow the road 2 km into Fermoy.

The town was founded at the end of the 18th century by John Anderson, a Scottish merchant settler, who gave land on the north side of the river to the British Army to build large barracks; much of the town's business was founded on meeting the needs of the garrison, which became one of the largest British Army centres in Ireland.

When you reach the bridge in the town, which dates from 1689, head downstream along Mill Road. After a few minutes, as the road bears right, continue along a narrow path beside a short millrace once associated with the great corn mills that lined the quays here. Cross a fence and head across a field to reach a footbridge over a tributary. Soon the path enters a pleasant treed section of riverbank often frequented by anglers seeking the fine salmon the Blackwater boasts. Indeed, it must be a most enjoyable experience to fish here; little flights of stone-paved steps have been built down to the water's edge in places, and seats are provided overlooking the river under the shelter of the great trees.

The pathway weaves its way along the steep-sided riverbank between tall trees, and shortly after the river bends around to the left, a great rusty viaduct spanning the river carrying the defunct Mallow and Fermoy Railway comes into sight, as if floating above the canopy of the trees. The stone piers of the viaduct, draped in long tendrils of ivy, seem to be growing out of the sheer 15 m cliff-face. On top of the cliff and close to the railway line are the ruins of Carrigabrick Castle, which can be accessed by clambering up a steep pathway, not to be recommended if you have vertigo! There is no record of when this castle was built, but from its circular shape, the thickness of its walls and the lack of a fireplace, it is reasonable to assume it was already a few hundred years old when one of its walls and the stairs were blown up by Cromwellians.

The trees are left behind as you climb a stile and follow an anglers' path along the edge of a field. In the distance ahead, over the wooded far bank, the blue-grey summits of the Knockmealdown Mountains can be glimpsed; overlooking the Blackwater from a high clearing is a fine double bow-fronted house. The waters of the river are slow moving here, and the surface was glass-like when I passed, disturbed only by the frequent leaping of large fish out in the middle and an agitated rippling close to the banks made by a host of tiny young fish. Along this stretch I disturbed a heron and two kingfishers that had obviously been attracted by these young fry.

About 35 minutes after leaving Fermoy you will reach a sign stating 'Fermoy Game Fishing Association — Private — All Fishing Preserved'. This is the eastern limit of our walk, and time to turn about to return to the town. When you enter the wooded section of riverbank again, keep an eye out for a pathway leading up to the left; if you would prefer an alternative route back, this will take you to the public road, where you turn right to reach the main street within 10 minutes.

♦ WALK 4: THE RIVER BLACKWATER AT LISMORE, CO. WATERFORD ♦

Lismore is the finest of the Blackwater towns, a well-preserved and picturesque place gathered about the walled and wooded grounds of Lismore Castle. St Carthage founded a monastery here in A.D. 636, and the place developed as a great centre of learning, attracting students from all over western Europe, one of whom was Alfred the Great of England. At one time the university town boasted of seven churches; today only fragments remain, some of which can be seen incorporated into St Carthage's Cathedral, dating from the 17th century, and the castle, which was substantially reconstructed in the 19th century to designs by Joseph Paxton, whose better-known works include the original Crystal Palace in London. This walk follows in the footsteps of a certain Lady Louisa down to the river's edge and along for 1.3 km, before looping around to return by the road.

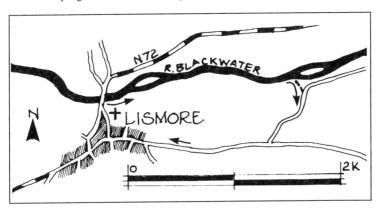

Walking time: 1 hour circuit
Terrain: Riverside paths, some a little rough, boreen and tarmac road.
How to get there: Lismore is on the N72, 27 km east of Fermoy, Co. Cork.
Map: OS Half-inch Sheet 22

Just south of Lismore bridge, below the castellated towers of the castle, go through a gate on to a pathway that takes you down under a canopy of trees along a rocky cliff-face high above the slow-flowing Blackwater. The far bank of the river has a row of stately poplars, while horse and

Spanish chestnut trees of huge girth and giant beeches line the path you walk. Beyond the poplars on the far bank and a broad meadow is the Lismore canal, completed in 1814 by the Duke of Devonshire. The Blackwater was already navigable from the sea to just above Cappoquin, and this section of canal enabled boats to come all the way to Lismore. It fell into disuse before the end of the 19th century, but was briefly in commission again in 1922 when the railway line between Cappoquin and Lismore was disrupted during the Civil War.

After a few minutes the path takes you through a gate into a field; to shorten the walk you can turn right here up a lane that will return you to the town. A sometimes indistinct path takes you along the riverbank now; be careful not to disturb the crop in the field. When I passed here in late July the riverbank was a mass of tall colourful Himalayan balsam, attended to by clouds of tortoiseshell butterflies, more than I can ever remember seeing in one place. Further on the balsam had extended right into the field making a magnificent display.

The river here crosses noisily over a series of rapids, skirting a midstream island. Crossing a metal bridge the walk continues along the edge of a beet field. Stay close to the riverbank, but take care not to stand at the edge because of frequent collapses of the sandy soil.

A stile is reached and crossed into a field where the path is a little less distinct than it has been, and boggy in places; the town is left far behind now and there is not a house to be seen. This stretch of the river is called the Bishop's Fishery, a name that harks back to Norman times. The island in the river is called Bullsod Island. Another stile leads you on to a good path through a wooded section of the riverbank. About 30 minutes after setting out, some stone steps are descended leading to a narrow and ancient boreen that goes right and away from the river. This is the end of the walk; to get back to Lismore you have a choice of retracing your steps or following the boreen, which will take you to the public road.

Ascend the boreen between overgrown stone walls; behind the wall on the right now is a wooded hill called locally Round Hill. It is not a completely natural hill, but a great earthwork anciently called *Dunsginne*, probably an Iron Age military or ceremonial site. It is this structure, called in the time of St Carthage *An Lois Mór* (the great enclosure), that gave the town of Lismore its name. This is probably the largest prehistoric earthwork in County Waterford, and originally the enclosure on the summit was surrounded by a double-ring of moat-like trenches. The boreen you follow, and the road beyond, is part of *An Rian Bó Phádraig*, the ancient highway of the Decies, which dates back to at least early Christian times, so you walk in the company of the shades of centuries of travellers. It is possible that travellers originally crossed the river here by a ford or a timber bridge.

Turn right on to the public road, met a few minutes later, and shortly after, at the next junction, right again. Over across the wooded Blackwater valley now the pyramidic summit of the Knockmealdown Mountains forms the backdrop to the scene.

After about 20 minutes Lismore is entered; turn right down Church Lane, a narrow street of beautiful old and new cottages, and bear left around a little green towards the church spire. The ornate gateway to St Carthage's Cathedral beckons you in; it is a beautiful and historic Gothic church well worth a visit.

Past the gates descend a stone-walled laneway to reach the road 100 m south of the bridge.

THE RIVER BOYNE

Far back in the murky mists of time, the goddess Boand displeased the spirits of the underworld, and three great tidal waves burst out of the earth to seek out and drown her. Boand was swift, however, and she escaped east to the coast near Drogheda, where the waves were swallowed by the sea. Boand's ultimate fate is unclear, but the waters remaining after the passage of the three waves became the River Boyne. It is a majestic river that rises near Edenderry and meanders for 110 km through fine and fertile countryside before it reaches the sea near Drogheda. The quieter reaches of the river, particularly the woodland parts, are a bird lover's paradise; in spring and summer the dawn chorus is a day-long event.

The Boyne Navigation Company began work to link up towns like Navan and Trim with the sea in 1748, and over the following fifty years a series of bypassing canals was built to avoid the worst rapids. The scheme was never a commercial success, however, and regular passenger-carrying and transport of goods ceased early in the 20th century. We are fortunate today to have the legacy the company left, a series of towpaths from Drogheda to Trim; many stretches are at time of writing not traversable with ease, but it seems that, eventually, it will be possible to walk the whole way. In the meantime I describe below three walks that sum up the best of the Boyne.

♦ WALK 5: THE RIVER BOYNE: FROM DROGHEDA TO NEWGRANGE, CO. MEATH ♦

This walk is a good introduction to the beauties of this fine river. It is a walk rich in flora and fauna, in addition to a historical background that spans 5,000 years and ranges from the great tombs of the neolithic past to the fateful Battle of the Boyne, when a Dutchman defeated a

Scotsman to win the crown of England! Hopefully, a footbridge connection will be made between the towpath and the new Boyne Valley Heritage Centre, which is being completed at time of writing, which will allow you to end your walk with a visit to the centre and by another bridge to the Newgrange monument itself. In the absence of a link to the heritage centre, if you don't wish to do a 'there and back' and can arrange a pick-up or a group with two cars, you can access, through a farmyard with the permission of the occupants, the public road west of the village of Donore.

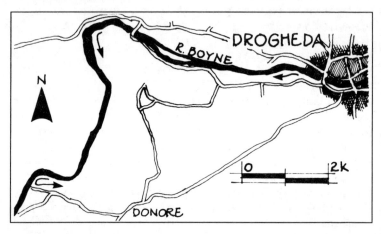

Walking time: 3½ hours to the Boyne Valley Heritage Centre; 7 hours there and back
Terrain: Varies from tarmac to grand grassy towpaths to often overgrown and muddy riverside paths.
How to get there: Drogheda is on the N1, 48 km north of Dublin. There is plenty of parking near the most western bridge in the town crossing the river, which is where the walk starts.
Map: OS Half-inch Sheet 13

The walk starts on the south side of the River Boyne in Drogheda, where a tarmac path drops down to the riverbank opposite the historic town, which rises up the far bank to a skyline of grey-slated roofs, church spires and towers. Underneath the modern bridge the blandness of its concrete is enlivened by some astonishing, colourful and amusing graffiti.

On the west side of the bridge, opposite a great disused flax mill, a gravel path leads out into the countryside. The river is very broad and slow flowing here, and has allowed an extensive reed-bed to develop on the north bank; constant calls of waterfowl when I passed indicated it must be a fine habitat for wildlife. Its closeness to the sea and the tidal nature of this stretch ensures that among the water birds you are likely to see is the cormorant, either cruising along the water's surface, hull down, taking frequent dives, or swiftly flying centimetres above the river, with strong purposeful wing-beats.

The Boyne now flows between banks that become increasingly high on both sides. To the left the incline is so steep that its grasses have never been introduced to fertiliser, and in springtime it displays a grand show of primroses, while at the river's edge great clumps of marsh marigolds raise their splendid glowing yellow cups to the light.

Soon the spired skyline of Drogheda recedes behind and the riverside path reaches a tarmac road. In the future I hope the authorities will develop a separate pathway along the water's edge, but for now we have to put up with this stretch on tarmac. The margins of the road are lined with butterbur, once used as a cure for 'plague and pestilence'. Its early-blooming flowers are valuable to bee-keepers as a source of nectar at a time of scarcity, and it is often found at rivers' edges because it was originally planted there to stabilise the earth of the banks with its matting roots, so hated by gardeners.

Nearly an hour after setting out, the first part of the old Boyne navigation, the Oldbridge canal, is reached, where a section of the river's rapids is bypassed. The work on the lock was completed in 1778, and it was in use into the early years of the 20th century; in the summertime pleasure boats plied from here to Slane in time for lunch before returning. The old gates are sadly rotting away now, but the stones of the lock await a reawakening. The old lockhouse still survives, well extended and refurbished, opposite the lock.

Shortly after passing Oldbridge lock, the road turns sharply right at the gates of the Oldbridge demesne. A fine lodge inside the gates displays a stone carved with the date 1690, which does not necessarily refer to the date it was built, but more likely commemorates the Battle of the Boyne fought near by. One of the generals on William's side, the Duke of Schomberg, was killed in the battle and is said to have been buried near where the lodge stands.

A bridge takes the road across the canal, and the sound of the rapids on the river beyond a curtain of woodland can be heard again. At a ford near here in July 1690 the main action of the Boyne's famous battle took place.

The protagonists were the Catholic James II of England and his Protestant daughter's Dutch husband, William of Orange. William led an army that included Dutch, Danish and German soldiers, as well as English, and outnumbered, out-gunned and out-generalled James's army of Irish and French. William took an active part in the battle, being slightly wounded at one stage, but James apparently spent the day praying in the chapel at Donore a couple of kilometres away, before fleeing south with a bodyguard as his army made an orderly retreat from the battlefield. An obelisk commemorating the battle, which used to stand on an outcrop of rock at the northern side of the bridge, was blown up in the 1920s.

Staying on the south side of the bridge, follow a muddy track along the canal. To the left across the canal is a small mangrove-like swamp beyond which are the tall redwoods, cypresses and limes of the Oldbridge demesne, and soon the grey limestone three-storey facade of 18th-century Oldbridge House comes into view. An overgrown shrubbery of rhododendrons, laurel and cherry trees was in full and gloriously fragrant flower when I passed, and I was entertained by grey squirrels leaping through the branches.

Look out along here for an ivy-clothed concrete pillbox built during World War II, presumably to dissuade foreign forces from using the river. An old stone bridge is crossed shortly after to return you on to the south side of the canal, and further on an elaborate old fish-weir on the river is passed.

Soon a milestone on the towpath indicates you are 4 miles (6 km) from the bridge at Drogheda, and further on the limestone bedrock is exposed where the river has cut a way through it. Wild cherry trees, probably escapees from a nearby demesne, decorate the broad woodland wilderness through which the river passes now. High up to the left the ruin of a bow-fronted house called Farm peers out from the trees.

When I walked there, the track became a bit rough and very boggy shortly after. The worst of this problem section can be avoided by ascending a staircase, built from railway sleepers cut into the cliffside, and at the top turning right through a field and shortly after descending again on to the riverbank.

Soon after the path improves again and takes you along a magnificent slow-flowing reach of river margined with yellow flags and giant marsh marigolds and enclosed by woodland and grassy hills. After a sharp bend in the river, just out of view on the wooded hill on the far side, Dowth, the first of the three great neolithic monuments that line the Boyne, is passed.

After a while the next section of canal is reached at Staleen; note how the stones of the lock are being lifted by an ash tree that has gained a precarious hold in a mortar joint. At the next bridge the occupier of the adjacent lockhouse has turned the overgrown canal in front of the house into a beautiful water garden. Cross the bridge here and continue along the long, narrow 'island' between the canal and the river, through a pleasant tunnel of hawthorn and ivy.

Close to the next bridge you will find a stone noting that you are 10 km from Drogheda. If you turn left here and walk away from the canal, you can pass through a farmyard (do seek permission if possible) to reach the public road that will bring you to the village of Donore within about 30 minutes. You can, however, continue on for a further 5 minutes to reach the Boyne Valley Heritage Centre and get a view across the river to Newgrange, the finest of the neolithic monuments. At time of writing, there is no access from the towpath to the centre, but it is hoped that such will be provided.

♦ WALK 6: THE RIVER BOYNE: FROM SLANE TO CARRICKDEXTER WEIR, CO. MEATH ♦

This short but splendid walk along the Boyne takes you upstream to pass under Slane Castle and enter a deep woodland-clothed ravine. A 19th-century guidebook gushed that a voyage up this section would make one 'nothing worse than a pillar of admiration' for the surroundings.

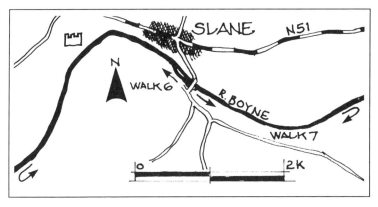

Walking time: 1½ hours there and back
Terrain: Varying from grand grassy towpaths to often overgrown and sometimes muddy riverside paths.
How to get there: Slane is on the N51, 14 km from Drogheda.
Maps: OS Half-inch Sheet 13

On the west side of Slane bridge cross a stile into a broad, grassy field and head diagonally across it to where the river roars over a long weir. Straight ahead the village church tower rises from the woodland of the Slane Castle demesne, which forms a dense treed edge to the far side of the river. Passing the weir and its water, flowing glass-like and smooth into a churning turbulence, continue along the river's edge. In the distance, Slane Castle is glimpsed on a height above the Boyne.

After about 15 minutes a short section of navigation canal and the remains of Slane Castle lock are reached. Over to the left, almost taken over by trees and shrubs, are the sad remains of the particularly quaint lockhouse. In spring and summer this area can be alive with pheasants, bred on the estate for the shooting season. Out of season I have found these exotic birds can be surprisingly unconcerned at the approach of humans, but as soon as the shooting season begins, they seem to melt into the countryside!

Beyond the lock, look out for a stile that will take you over a fence and down along a muddy path through thick undergrowth to the river-bank.

The path emerges at the water's edge near another roaring weir overlooked by Slane Castle. A castle was originally built here at what was then the perimeter of Dublin's Pale by the Flemings in the 15th century, and is apparently contained within the existing extensive building. The lands around Slane came into the hands of the Conyngham family after the Battle of the Boyne, in which Sir Albert Conyngham took part, and about 1785 the present castle was built to the designs of James Wyatt and completed by Francis Johnston, although such luminaries as Capability Brown and James Gandon are also mentioned in its connection. It was seriously damaged by fire in 1991, and although the present owner, Lord Mountcharles, has restoration works in progress, there were still many sad and gaping blackened windows when I passed.

A narrow and sometimes precarious pathway takes you along the river's edge between a rocky cliff, festooned in ivy, ferns and woodbine, and the water. Take care here; it can be very slippery after wet weather and it would not be difficult to slide into the water!

About 30 minutes after setting out, a deep, steep-sided and heavily treed valley is entered, through which the broad Boyne winds slowly and majestically. Cliff-like limestone escarpments rise high above the grassy towpath, the most spectacular of which, whitened with lichen, is called Maiden Rock. A little further on an old redwood tree growing on a tiny island in the middle of the river provides a favourite roosting place for cormorants, where they can hang out their wings to dry.

At a gateway in the remains of an old stone wall you pass into the Beauparc demesne which, like Slane Castle, is owned by Lord Mountcharles. Soon the great V-shaped weir at Carrickdexter lock, the turn-around point of this walk, is reached. It is a good place to sit and admire the river in its woodland setting before returning to Slane bridge. Beyond the trees on the far side of the river the ruins of Carrickdexter Castle, once a significant fortress, can be glimpsed. The Beauparc demesne is planted with a rich variety of tall classic trees and contrasts well with the natural scrub woodland passed since leaving

Slane bridge. Beauparc House itself, a bow-fronted Georgian mansion, is perched high up in the trees above the bend of the river and must enjoy the finest views on the Boyne.

◆ WALK 7: THE RIVER BOYNE: FROM SLANE TO ROSNAREE LOCK, CO. MEATH ◆

This is a short river walk along the towpath between the old canal, now partially colonised by rushes, flags and small shrubs, and the broad Boyne, ending at a ruined lockhouse at the Rosnaree lock on the old navigation.

See the map on p. 15.

Walking time: 1 hour there and back
Terrain: Comfortable grassy towpaths, sometimes a little muddy in places.
How to get there: Slane is on the N51, 14 km from Drogheda.
Map: OS Half-inch Sheet 13

The walk starts at the south side of Slane bridge; there is a handy car park right at the bridge. Cross a stile and follow the old towpath alongside the linear water garden the canal has become. The large and fine limestone-faced building across the river is Slane Mill, built in 1766 to store, kiln dry and grind cereal into flour, which it accomplished at a rate of 17,000 barrels per year. Uphill to the right the gaunt ruin of Fennor Castle rises from a grove of trees.

Soon a tree-covered and weed-festooned series of outcrops in the river is reached; this is what remains of a substantial eel-weir called Cherry Island.

In a short time you have left roads and buildings completely behind and you follow a comfortable track through a countryside of gentle grassy hills scattered with islands of yellow gorse. Speedwell, celandine and primroses made a colourful margin to the track, while the outcrops of blackthorns along the way were hung down with frothy bursts of May blossom when I passed here.

About 20 minutes after setting out, and as the towpath becomes enclosed by bushes and trees, look out on the right for the Scraggy Arch, a place where the canal had to be cut through solid bedrock, creating a short tunnel-like arch. It is interesting to see how common ivy has colonised the much-fissured rock and is sundering it bit by bit, squeezing into and filling every crevice and crack with serpentine sinews, wrapping itself round and round and upwards to where it pushes out a canopy of leaves.

Further along the pathway becomes a bit muddy as it passes by the incongruous sight of two old motor cars resting on the bottom of the canal. Half an hour after setting out, the ivy-roofed ruined lockhouse at Rosnaree is reached.

It is at Rosnaree that a 3rd-century high king, Cormac Mac Airt, father-in-law to Finn Mac Cumhaill, is said to be buried. After a forty-year reign in pre-Patrician Ireland, it is said that he became a Christian before he died and wished to be buried, not in the old pagan royal necropolis of *Brú na Bóinne*, but on the south side of the river at Rosnaree. After his death (he is said to have choked on a salmon bone, but he was more likely poisoned) his priests were unwilling to carry out his wishes, but try as they might, the corps of warriors carrying his bier across the ford to the brugh were forced back by the waters until eventually a wave swept the bier away downstream to deposit it at Rosnaree.

You may return to Slane bridge the way you came, or if the river is not high, follow the anglers' path along the river's edge all the way.

◆ WALK 8: THE CLARE RIVER, CO. TIPPERARY ◆

The Clare river rises on the western slopes of Mauherslieve in County Tipperary and, flowing westwards, cuts deep into a geological fault in the old red sandstone bedrock to form a wonderful gorge known as the Clare Glens. The gorge forms the border between Counties Limerick and Tipperary, and in 1927 it was donated by its owner as a public amenity to the two local authorities.

The marvellous waterfalls created by the river as it descends from the hills, the mossy trees and shrubs overhanging the gorge, and the winding pathways following the river make for an exciting woodland walk. In addition to the walk described below, there is a Nature Trail about 1.5 km long.

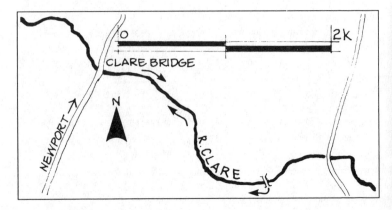

Walking time: 1½ hours round trip
Terrain: Pathways varying from narrow and muddy to soft leafy woodland tracks.
How to get there: The Clare Glens are well signposted 3 km from the small town of Newport, Co. Tipperary, which is 16 km east of Limerick city on the R503.
Map: OS Half-inch Sheet 18

Leaving the car park, walk south 100 m to Clare Bridge; turn left through a gate on to a path following the river. Near the entrance gate a mapboard shows the layout of the glens.

The river cascades noisily down a boulder-filled watercourse bordered here by a coniferous wood. Steps take you up the side of the gorge; keep right to stay close to the river's edge, where you will descend steps carved from the sandstone to continue along broad flat pavements of the rock. The river bursts over ledges to crash into deep pools; its flow slows down for a short distance before it reaches another drop and rushes ahead again.

The gorge gets deeper as you proceed until cliffs of pink sandstone, overhung with beech and ash trees garlanded with woodbine and ivy, tower sheer above. The moist atmosphere encourages a rich herbarium including, when I walked there, stitchwort, wood sorrel, lady's lace, hart's-tongue ferns, celandine, dead nettle, mosses of all descriptions and many species I was unable to name. The shapes formed in the sandstone by the water as it plummets over little cliffs are fascinating; in one place the configuration of the rock turns the flow into a spectacular glistening fan.

Keep a close eye on the pavements you walk on; in places the surface has ripple marks, the same as you will see on many a modern beach, but these were formed when the rock still consisted of loose grains of sand over 300 million years ago.

Nearly 15 minutes after setting out you come to two much bigger waterfalls, and turn up steps to your left through fraughan bushes and rhododendrons. If you want to make a detour to get close to one of the biggest cascades, drop down again to the right a little further on and descend to the riverside. Take care; where they are wet the rock surfaces can be slippery, and in this place, with the air permanently very moist, they are always wet. This waterfall is more than 3 m high, pouring over a Giant's Causeway of columnar rock. Retrace your steps to the main path and continue uphill, turning right at the top to cross a concrete bridge.

The roaring of the river has been almost left behind up here, but it can still be seen through a screen of rhododendrons and laurels. Keeping right on the path leads you back to the river near a bridge that will bring you to the far side from where you can return to the start if you wish. Continuing on, the path runs through a leafy-floored tunnel of laurels and rhododendrons, some twisted and gnarled into fantastic shapes, and briefly away from the river again. There are many opportunities to stop and take it all in; this walk would not be complete without at least one such stop.

About 30 minutes after setting out the path is interrupted by a fence; cross the fence and continue through an entirely different kind of wood, an ancient hazel grove carpeted in wood anemone. The path forks here: the main route continues straight (the left fork); while bearing right will bring you down again across rugged terrain to the water's edge. There are some pools here where in hot weather it is hard to resist having a swim.

Following the main route, however, after about 10 minutes the path descends to reach a bridge over a deep, canal-like section of the river with sheer rock sides below a tall waterfall. A gravel path continues a little further upstream past an ancient holy well, until it ends abruptly at a hedge, the turning-back point. Returning, stay on the south side of the river; except for two stiles, the pathway is broad and even all the way, taking you high above the gorge back to the public road.

◆ WALK 9: THE CONG RIVER AND LOUGH CORRIB, CO. GALWAY ◆

Between Lough Mask and Lough Corrib lies a narrow strip of land that is as rich in natural beauty as it is in historic and prehistoric remains. The hub of this area, straddling the border with County Mayo, is the village of Cong, still trumpeting its fame as the location for the 1950s movie, *The Quiet Man*, and the nearby Ashford Castle, a 19th-century Scottish baronial mansion turned luxury hotel.

There are many excellent walks around Cong; this one combines the shores of Lough Corrib with the banks of the 1 km-long, picturesque Cong river. This walk, and all the others available in the area, has lots of jungle-like stretches, ruins and caves that children in particular will find fascinating.

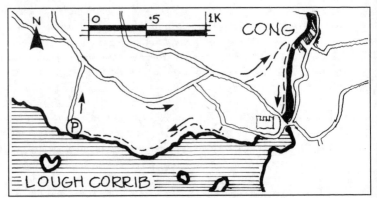

Walking time: 2 hours
Terrain: Tarmac forestry road, gravel tracks, and riverside paths, suitable for all.
How to get there: The village of Cong is on the R345, 11 km south of the town of Ballinrobe.
Map: OS Discovery Series Sheet 38

Driving west out of the village of Cong, turn left at the Clonbur junction; 2 km further on, turn left on to a side road. After 750 m turn right at a junction to reach, near the shore of Lough Corrib, a car park provided by Coillte, who look after a large part of the original Ashford Castle grounds.

Walk back the way you came along the road through the woods; Lough Corrib is left behind as the road leads you inland. At a T-junction turn right, and after a few minutes the Deer Park lake can be seen through the trees to the left, its surface covered with water lilies when I passed.

About 25 minutes after starting out, a picturesque gate lodge is reached and the road passes between two great stone piers. Just beyond the gates there is a long straight terraced walk that leads directly down to Ashford Castle. Keep on straight and at the next junction bear around to the right to reach the Ashford Equestrian Centre. Leave the tarmac and go left around the centre to follow a track into the trees.

Soon you are passing through a dark green tunnel of laurels and beeches; keep on straight although you may see the Cong river glinting down to your right. After about 10 minutes you will reach a Y-junction; go right and after a few moments slip down a pathway to join the river path and turn right along it.

The sometimes muddy pathway meanders along a swampy tributary fringed with reed banks and tall spears of purple loosestrife for a few minutes before it reaches the Cong river, which is an unusual watercourse. Lough Mask drains into Lough Corrib, the surface of which is nearly 7 m lower, by a series of underground streams that unify near the village of Cong and come to the surface as the Cong river. The porous nature of the limestone around the southern shores of Lough Mask that causes this phenomenon should have been a warning to the engineers who attempted to construct a canal connecting the two lakes in the 1840s. It was felt that for the cost of a canal of only 6 km in length, a trading route of 80 km in length encompassing the two great lakes with a direct connection to the sea at Galway could be opened up. For five years the work proceeded, giving welcome employment to a peasantry beset by famine. Try as they might, however, the engineers could not prevent the porous bedrock from draining the canal, and when it became clear that the northern end would be permanently dry, the project was abandoned. You can still follow much of the course of this ill-fated canal between the two lakes, past beautifully constructed but dry locks and harbours.

Soon after reaching the Cong river, a Gothic-arched gateway is reached which leads to a bridge over the river to an island and a picturesque ruin called the Monks' Fishing House. This 12th-century building was associated with nearby Cong Abbey and probably controlled an ancient fish-weir on the river. The 19th-century arches of the gateways leading to the bridge have keystones representing the heads of the last abbot of Cong Abbey and of Roderick O'Connor, the last high king of Ireland, who died here in 1198 having spent the final years of his life as a monk.

Continue along the west bank of the river through a tunnel of laurels with twisted trunks and branches, where great slabs of limestone bedrock protrude from the ground, making a background like something out of a scary Disney cartoon. A roaring weir on the river is passed after which the waters calm and become glass-like, reflecting the foliage of the far bank.

Shortly after, the path leaves the trees behind quite suddenly, and the vast array of towers and pinnacles of Ashford Castle fills the scene ahead. Built originally about 1750 as a hunting lodge, it was enlarged in the 19th century by the Guinness family.

Walk around the right side of the castle and continue across to reach a tarmac pathway running to the right near to and parallel to the shore of Lough Corrib. It is a substantial body of water measuring about 32 km from north to south, not as big as but certainly longer than Lough Neagh. An old boathouse is passed on the left, a stone building with a roof of massive slates, and there are frequent glimpses through the trees of the lake scattered with its many thickly wooded islands. A more modern and certainly less picturesque boathouse is passed soon after. The forest has a rich variety of trees, including yew, holly, and hazel from which ripe nuts were dropping when I passed.

After about 15 minutes the path bears around to the right, but you should go left following a gravel path and a sign that states 'Chalet Walk and Bathing Place'. In summertime the rhododendrons and all the deciduous trees and shrubs enclose the path darkly, with the lake only glinting now and then off to the left. It can be heard, though, as it splashes on the rocky shore, particularly if the wind is from the south.

On the right look out for a plant not commonly seen in such abundance, the bamboo, with its broad, long leaves and green-sheathed stalks. Be vigilant for a narrow pathway going left off the main path; follow it down to the shore to reach a small cove which I am told is popular for swimming and sunbathing in summertime.

Cross the cove and follow the narrow leafy pathway as it wends its way through a thick woodland and then a low tunnel of holly and rhododendron. At the end of the tunnel swing around to the right and up a little meadow field to reach the tarmac road beside the car park, the starting point of this walk. Before finishing, however, turn right to reach a stone obelisk and Lady Olive's Chalet.

The chalet, a mock-rustic structure with a great limestone fireplace, was built by Lord Ardilaun in 1908 as a tea house for his wife. Ardilaun was a member of the Guinness family and a seriously rich landowner; he inherited Ashford Castle from his father in 1868, together with thousands of acres of land between Loughs Corrib and Mask, and spent much of his life 'improving' this and other properties, which included St Anne's in Raheny in Dublin.

If you stand just under the porch of the chalet and stamp your feet, the bats that occupy the roofspace above will start twittering. The nearby obelisk, raised by Lady Olive in memory of her husband, looks incongruous in scale and design beside the chalet. The view out across the lake from here is wonderful. Of the two near islands, the bigger one to the right is called Ardilaun (the high island), and it was from this that Lord Ardilaun took his name.

♦ WALK 10: THE DARGLE RIVER AT POWERSCOURT, CO. WICKLOW ♦

The Dargle river rises in the Wicklow Mountains and after descending abruptly by way of a dramatic waterfall that has been a tourist attraction for 250 years, it slows down and meanders through Powerscourt demesne, full of great exotic trees, many planted 200 years ago by the 2nd Viscount Powerscourt.

This walk follows the course of the Dargle for almost 2 km to Ballinagee bridge. Most visitors to Powerscourt spend their time in the formal gardens, so this walk is much less frequented. There is a charge to enter the demesne, but it is well worth it if you spend a day there. The opening hours are long (9.30 a.m. to 5.30 p.m., March to October), there is a nice café, a book shop with plenty of reasonably priced specialist guides to the place, a good children's playground, and there is more than enough to see to fill a week!

Time: 1¼ hours plus options
Terrain: Macadam private road all the way, but with a 20 minute woodland path option.
How to get there: Powerscourt demesne is 1 km outside the village of Enniskerry, Co. Wicklow, 15 km south of Dublin.
Map: OS Discovery Series Sheet 56

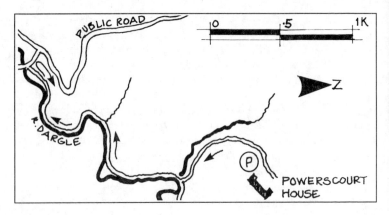

From the car park, rather than entering the formal gardens go right and then left and follow a sign for Riverside Walks. Follow the rhododendron- and laurel-bordered road as it descends steeply with great old beech and oak trees forming a canopy overhead. In a few minutes you will hear, as a background to the birdsong, the sound of rushing water coming from the undergrowth to the right, telling you the Dargle is not far away. The oaks and beeches give way soon to towering redwoods, related to the giant sequoias of the American Pacific coast, which are amongst the tallest trees in the world. To get a real feeling for the size of these redwoods, you need to stand right beneath one, back to the trunk, and gaze up towards the top. The gnarled bark is surprisingly soft and warm to the touch; it provides the tree with thermal insulation against forest fires in its native habitat.

After less than 10 minutes the Dargle river is reached at a T-junction; turn right and follow the river upstream, crossing a wild garlic-trimmed bridge over the cascading tributary heard earlier. The road bends around and becomes an avenue bounded by towering and elegant giant redwoods. There are lots of excellent locations along here with picnic tables at which to take a break and just watch the river go by.

Soon after, the formality of the avenue is left behind as the road enters an area of wilderness woodland, a conglomeration of oaks, sycamores, beeches, rhododendrons and laurels. Among the less common birds I saw here were the tiny goldcrest, moving swiftly along branches, and the white-breasted tree creeper, which circles the trunks of trees in search of insects. Keep an eye out as the road bears around to the left for a leafy pathway leading away to the bank of the river, and leave the road to follow it.

The path, scattered with pine needles and cones, is a great place for young children to explore; it is like a jungle track meandering along a riverbank, passing alternately through clearings full of dappled sunlight and dark shaded tunnels through shrubs. Early in the morning look out for red squirrels here; when I passed, the ground was littered with pine cones that had been stripped by them to get at the seeds.

Every so often the river is lined with a short sandy beach, the fine sand made up of fragments of degraded granite. The usual birds are less frequently seen in the coniferous areas of the woods here, but foraging dippers and grey wagtails are common along this stretch of the river.

Soon a bridge comes into view ahead signalling the end of the walk. Follow the riverbank around to a second bridge to reconnect with the tarmac road you left a short time earlier; you may retrace your steps along the riverbank or return by the road.

Back at the T-junction, where the river was first met, you can extend this walk by continuing straight to reach the Tinehinch Gates (20 minutes there and back). Otherwise you can return to walk through the formal gardens which are amongst the finest in Europe. They include an Italian garden, a Japanese garden, ornamental lakes and a pets' cemetery, a circuit of which will take about another hour of walking time.

THE RIVER DODDER

The River Dodder and the River Liffey are born in granite and come to the peaty surface within a short distance of each other under the Dublin Mountains' highest summit, Kippure. The Liffey flows towards the south but is blocked from the Irish Sea by the bulk of the Wicklow Mountains, and so flows a roundabout way towards the west, and then north, and finally east before entering Dublin Bay after a journey of 138 km. The Dodder, rising just over the brow of the hill from the Liffey, finds its way more directly to the bay after only 29 km. Short and all as it is, the Dodder's mountain catchment area ensures that on occasions it causes consternation when it delivers, with little warning, prodigious amounts of turf-stained water into the south side of Ireland's capital city. I describe two contrasting walks along this short-tempered but beautiful stream, one in the surrounds of its mountain beginnings, and the other as it wends its way, sometimes secretly, through Dublin's suburbs.

♦ WALK 11: THE RIVER DODDER AT KIPPURE, CO. DUBLIN ♦

This is a short exhilarating mountain walk following the infant Dodder up through a deep ravine and out on to high open treeless moorland; although very close to a road at all times, one gets a real feeling of being in a remote wilderness; not to be recommended if you are inexperienced in mountain walking and visibility is either bad or threatening to become bad.

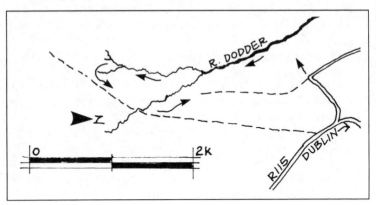

Walking time: 2¼ hours (allow about an extra hour if you are going to take on Kippure). Climb 160 m (plus an extra 200 m for Kippure).

Terrain: The first half is on rough and rugged sheep tracks, sometimes quite boggy, through heather; the return is along a rough bog road.

How to get there: Take the R115 south from Rathfarnham, Co. Dublin, past Killakee and on to the moorlands called the Featherbeds, or on the Discovery Series Sheet 56, Glassamucky. Eleven km from Rathfarnham Castle take a sharp turn down a side road to the right. After less than 1 km the road turns sharply right; park just after the bend, on the left.

Maps: OS Discovery Series Sheets 50 and 56

Head directly downhill towards the ravine through which the infant Dodder flows. It is a little boggy in places, but there are plenty of easy routes down between the clumps of heather and gorse. In a matter of minutes the road has been left far behind, and as the sound of rushing waters greets you, you drop steeply down into the Dodder Gorge, a deep, steep-sided cut through which the river flows fast, cascading over many waterfalls, overhung by ancient mountain ash trees.

Until you have seen it, you cannot appreciate how deep and extensive the ravine is. This secluded place and the hills about are the location of the 'Chase of Glenasmole', an ancient Gaelic poem that chronicles an epic deer hunt involving Finn Mac Cumhaill and his magic hounds, Bran and Sgeolan. In another epic poem of the period the giant blackbirds, rowan berries and ivy of Glenasmole are mentioned, but I must admit I saw none of these when I walked here. However, the riverbanks and the boulders scattered along the gorge are always hung down with a rich variety of lichens, herbs and ferns; the place, because of its seclusion and shelter, is an oasis for flora and fauna.

Downstream the Dodder passes through groves of mountain ash, birch and beech trees and vanishes under a thick bulbous canopy of rhododendrons at the boundary of Glenasmole Lodge. Turn left and head upstream along the gorge, passing many small cascades and deep pools that offer cooling dips in summertime. A path of sorts meanders through the heather and bracken beside the stream, but sometimes you have to depart from it to avoid steep cliff-like sides. The steepest part is called St Mary's Cliff, which is said to be where the legendary giant ivy grows; see if you can find it!

A constant but gentle ascent takes you up along the river until you emerge from the gorge, and Bohernabreena Reservoirs appear behind, reflecting mirror-like on calm days their surrounding trees and the sky. Ahead, the pair of television masts on Kippure, Dublin's highest mountain at 757 m, comes into view followed by the flat summit itself. A junction is reached where two streams come together. The one coming from the left is called Mairin's Brook; cross it where it narrows and continue along paths through the heather to follow the Dodder out on to open heather-covered hills. Looking east from here, you should be able to make out a tin hut near a bog road that runs parallel to the Dodder's course downstream. This bog road will be your return route.

Soon an incomparable panorama opens up. Off in the distance between the rusty-coloured hills, the plain of Dublin with some signs of habitation stretches into the north; otherwise you stand in the midst of a treeless rolling wilderness of granite hills. It is a remote place, although sometimes people can be seen cutting turf on the bog to the east. There may be some sheep about, but I have seen deer here, and the ubiquitous skylark, and I have frequently disturbed red grouse that feed on the abundant heather.

The Dodder dwindles as you climb; in one place it is possible to see where it has cut right down through a 1 m-deep layer of peat and 2 m of boulder clay to the granite bedrock below. Tributaries running into it are often under the peat; you will see places where the peat has collapsed exposing tiny underground rivers.

After walking for about 20 minutes beyond the junction with Mairin's Brook, it is time to return, unless the weather is good and you want to conquer Kippure which seems quite near now. (It will take about 30 minutes to climb the last 200 m to the great masts where brilliant views can be had of the Wicklow Mountains, the Blessington Lakes, and indeed, when the weather is clear, the mountains of Wales. From close to the top you will be able to see the return route described below.)

Veer around to the left and walk eastwards across the heather; in less than 500 m, after crossing a few more ravines, you will come to a 3 m-wide cutting running up the mountain from the north-east, a feature that coincides with the Dublin/Wicklow County border. Follow the cutting downhill where, after crossing a couple of brooks, it becomes a bog road. Keep on the bog road for a few minutes until you see the tin hut seen earlier, now downhill ahead to the left. Cross heather again and some recent peat cuttings towards it, until you reach another bog road parallel to the first. Follow it north for a little more than 1 km to reach the public road near where you started.

◆ WALK 12: THE RIVER DODDER: FROM TEMPLEOGUE TO CLONSKEAGH, CO. DUBLIN ◆

This walk follows the Dodder as it flows along what is often a deep cutting through a fascinating suburbia of tiny parks and ruined mills. You will be pleasantly surprised by the hidden delights along the way and the extraordinarily rich flora and fauna to be encountered.

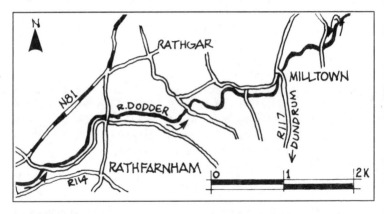

Walking time: 1½ hours one way, 3 hours there and back
Terrain: Gravel, tarmac and concrete paths, suitable for baby buggies.
How to get there: For this walk, the Dodder is accessed through Washington Park, a little estate off Butterfield Avenue (R114) in Templeogue, Co. Dublin.
Maps: OS Discovery Series Sheet 50; OS Dublin Street Guide, pp. 42 and 43

A walk of a few minutes through a well-landscaped housing estate brings you to meet a gravel path that takes you into the hidden world of the Dodder. A broad green space is before you with, a few hundred metres away, a picturesque crescent of granite and brick cottages. As you advance along the gravel path you realise that, between you and those cottages, the Dodder river runs, in a deep willow-cordoned cutting.

The path takes you along the south bank of the Dodder, a view of which is temporarily screened by a colourful and dense curtain of alders and willows. There are the makings of many wicker baskets here; you can see how easily harvested the thin and flexible 'sally' rods were in great numbers in the old days. Ahead a line of Lombardy poplars marks higher ground that diverts the course of the Dodder around to the left, and the limestone bed of the river is exposed, creating a series of little cascades and pools in which fish can be seen. Across the river where the houses now are was once a limestone quarry.

The path takes you under a modern graffiti-daubed bridge and high ground to the north diverts the river sharply around to the right. You emerge from under the bridge into a parkland with a rich variety of mature trees, the bushy oaks, sycamores, yews and chestnuts of the demesne of Bushy Park House. A footbridge takes you over to the north bank of the river, where the riverside path along the demesne wall (probably built from limestone quarried near by) is a most pleasant place to walk, particularly in autumn when the foliage is at its most colourful.

There is an informal screen of trees and shrubs between you and the river, made up mainly of willows, the bigger of which are called crack willows, from the brittle nature of their branches. Across the river on high ground can be seen the gable of the old medieval Rathfarnham church with its double-belfry, and the spire of the more modern church built in 1785. The riverside path ends at Rathfarnham bridge; make your way up to the road and cross over to Dodder Park Road, nip over a low wall and descend once more to the river, following a waterside promenade. If you are walking with a buggy continue along the pavement to join the riverbank further on.

The Dodder is usually glass-like here due to the weir a little further on, and produces wondrous reflections of the sheer cliff of foliage on the north bank, especially in autumn. Early in the morning a heron can often be seen standing sentry at the weir, while dippers flit back and forth. Waterhens and, if you are lucky, kingfishers are also present on this stretch. Soon the pathway rises to road level and you cross the river by a footbridge. The glorious Rathfarnham Castle gatehouse can be seen across the road. It was built in the 1770s by Viscount Ely, owner of Rathfarnham Castle, and indicates the extent of the castle demesne at that time; the castle itself is 1.5 km away. It contained living accommodation for a gatekeeper and was inhabited up to the 1940s.

The footbridge brings you into a little park where the path continues along a line of weeping willows bordering the river. The Dodder is quite slow moving now after a further weir near the footbridge, and it is here that you are likely to see kingfishers which, being very shy birds, are usually only glimpsed as an electric blue flash as they hurtle away. They have been known to nest in burrows in the south bank.

The river swings abruptly to the north again as if avoiding the wooded high ground ahead, on top of which Mount Carmel Hospital stands, and passes under a modern bridge that carries Orwell Road. Beyond the bridge on the south bank stands one of the most magnificent weeping willows I have ever seen, a piece of arboreal poetry. This is followed by a marvellous, wide curved weir where the river falls about 2.5 m. Just before the weir the remains of a millrace, where water was taken off the Dodder to drive a watermill, probably in the 18th century, can be seen.

The Dodder now runs through another little park and bears around yet again to the north in the face of high ground ahead. Our route takes us briefly away from the river as we follow a laneway up to the main road at Dartry, past the Dartry Dye Works, a fine late Victorian building of red brick and limestone. Further on there is another tiny park beside the Dropping Well pub, but at present Classon's bridge cannot be passed at river level, so I recommend you pass by the pub, cross the bridge to the south bank and continue along the river towards the railway viaduct. At the time of writing there are great changes occurring in this area. On the north bank blocks of apartments are being built on the site of the old Dartry Laundry, and soon the railway viaduct, which has lain unused for nearly forty-five years, will be back in use carrying passengers on a light rail system.

Passing under the viaduct the river runs through Milltown, named for the large number of watermills that once used the power of the Dodder's waters to carry out operations like grinding corn, sawing timber, milling iron and making paper. The narrow old bridge which once carried the Dundrum road is a pedestrian bridge today.

Cross the main road and follow a broad tarmac path that meanders with the river on the left and the demesne wall of castellated Clonskeagh Castle on the right. The river is fringed by Himalayan balsam, a very tall-standing flowering plant I have seen in places along the Barrow and Suir rivers. This is a very pleasant stretch, passing little bridges and arches, the purpose for which is lost in time.

At the next bridge you have come to the end of the parkland riverside walk; from now the river can only be followed along roadside pavement. Cross the road at Clonskeagh bridge and continue eastwards a little further along a pavement. To the right is a very modern industrial park built on the Beech Hill demesne, of which only the ornamental gateway remains.

Both riverbanks are heavily overgrown here as the Dodder narrows and veers away briefly and cascades over a broad waterfall. On the right after a modern development is Beaver Row, a fine terrace of thick-walled late Georgian cottages which overlook the river. Further on a footbridge will take you over to the north bank, which you can follow back past the waterfall to reach Clonskeagh Road beside Ashton's pub, a few hundred metres from Clonskeagh bridge.

◆ WALK 13: THE DOUGLAS RIVER, KILWORTH, CO. CORK ◆

The Douglas river rises in the foothills of the Kilworth mountains and flows south through a wooded glen extraordinarily rich in varieties of trees and plants to reach the Blackwater by way of the Araglin river.

In Walk 11, the Dodder river in the Dublin Mountains is followed across bare, infertile acid moorland to its source; the geology and surroundings of this walk, following a river of similar size, make for an extreme contrast. Late spring is probably the best time to take this walk, before the summer foliage hides all.

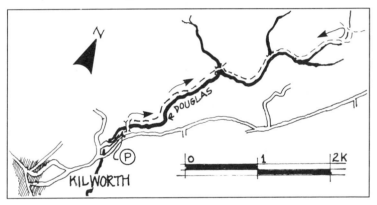

Walking time: 2 hours there and back
Terrain: Forestry tracks and paths, with a gentle climb some of the way, suitable for all.
How to get there: The village of Kilworth is on the R667, off the N8, 5 km north of Fermoy, Co. Cork.
Map: OS Half-inch Sheet 22

Take the road going east out of the village of Kilworth. After 1 km turn down to your left along a gravel track to meet and follow the narrow Douglas river into a wood. The river is crossed before you reach a picnic area a further 500 m along. Start your walk here, crossing the river again and following the gravel track as it passes through a spruce tree plantation, fringed with bracken and banks of rosebay willowherb when I passed. The river is out of sight now, but the sound of its susurrant waters percolates through the foliage.

Soon the spruce trees give way to a comfortable mixture of beech, oak, sycamores and the ubiquitous alder. Near the riverbank there are clumps of giant hogweed raising their creamy domes of flower high above the undergrowth.

As you reach junctions keep right; particular care is needed because left turns will take you into the firing ranges of the Kilworth Army camp. Where the river divides, cross a tributary coming from the left to follow the stream coming from the right and walk uphill along a steep-sided glen. The forestry track has been cut out of the hillside here, and when I passed the cutting was clothed in a lush growth of bracken, ferns and heather all intertwined with honeysuckle.

Note how the present-day river is tiny compared to what it was millennia ago; older banks, well back from today's water's edge, are very apparent in places. A little more than 30 minutes after setting out, a stone bridge is reached where the river divides again; here you can take a rest, sitting under a lone conifer to watch small fish jumping in the shade of the bridge. Some of the cobbles of red sandstone in the shallows can be seen to be covered with tiny clusters of grit; these are cases constructed from pebbles by caddis flies, to protect them in their larval state.

Turn right off the track after the bridge and follow a pathway up through the trees leaving the river far below. After a few minutes another forestry road is reached; turn right along it with views across the glen. The river is out of sight below, but soon it rises with the terrain, shrouded in undergrowth in summertime, to just below the level of the road. Just as sure as waterways such as this provide the right micro-environment for many plants, shrubs and trees, you can be sure to see a host of insects that thrive in the same zone. The most visible of these are usually the butterflies (I saw many ringlets, dark speckled woods and a few large rusty brown silver-washed fritillaries) and the damselflies. The most impressive, however, is the big hawker dragonfly which drones around like a model aircraft and seems almost as large!

As the road climbs further and the stream becomes more of a brook, different shrubs such as fraughans and broom replace those that were common lower down, and garlands of honeysuckle climb to the pinnacles of spruce trees that crowd in on the stream.

The brook now wends its way uphill, out of sight of the track much of the time, and in places bedrock forms its banks. About an hour after setting out, a T-junction in the track is reached. Go left, and after a minute or two another junction is reached; to the left, just below a tiny patch of grass and wildflowers, the Douglas river recedes from sight into the ground.

For a variation on the return, look out for a timber bridge across the river about two-thirds of the way back. Cross it and follow the heather-

and birch-lined pathway uphill high above the glen, with long views across to the Kilworth mountains, before it wends its way downhill, crossing a tributary to reach the picnic area and starting point by way of another bridge.

THE GLEN RIVER

The Glen river rises in the Mournes, north-west of Slieve Donard, Ulster's highest peak, and flows a little under 4 km to reach the sea at Dundrum Bay. It provides the route for an exhilarating walk that takes you up a hugely picturesque, rocky gorge into the open moorland of the Mourne Mountains. I also describe a longer walk which continues past the source of the Glen river to connect with the source of another short mountain stream, the Bloody Bridge river, and follows it to the sea.

◆ WALK 14: THE GLEN RIVER, CO. DOWN ◆

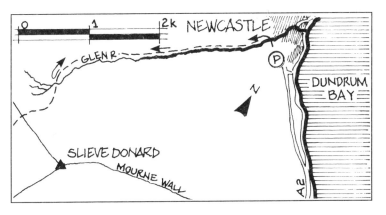

Walking time: 2¾ hours there and back

How to get there: Entering Newcastle from the south along the coast road, take the first turn left and uphill. Keep on straight until you reach a cul-de-sac at the entrance to the All Children's Integrated Primary School, where there is a small car park.

Terrain: A sometimes rough and steep riverside path with some boggy patches near the top; there is an ascent of about 450 m.

Map: NIOS Discoverer Series Sheet 29

An inconspicuous gap across the road from the school entrance gives on to a pathway through Donard Wood; follow it through glades of rhododendrons and tall ancient oaks, keeping on the main path and heading uphill. About 5 minutes after starting out, the splashing of the Glen river can be heard shortly before you reach a bridge.

Ascend beside the river as it sluices down around a series of erratic boulders. There is something very exotic about the scene; the combination of spiny conifers and stone gives the place an unmistakable Japanese feeling; it is like a continuous climbing rock garden. The water of the river is the clearest I have seen in a mountain river in Ireland, probably because this river is not draining a large area of peat uplands. Along its course the river sometimes disappears under great clumps of holly and rhododendrons, emerging to cascade into some deeply hollowed-out pools that would be heaven to dip into on a hot summer's day.

As you climb, glimpses of great views out over Dundrum Bay open up behind. A tall stone bridge with a date 1865 takes you across to the other side of the river where you continue uphill. Soon the top of Thomas's mountain, the northern spur of Slieve Donard, can be seen over the trees.

The bedrock you are walking on, laced and criss-crossed with stripes, is a shale which was laid down 350 million years ago and covered this whole area before it became eroded and the underlying granite was exposed; watch out as you ascend for a change to take place, the line where the granite bursts through. Above this line almost all the rocks you see will be granite, although in the western Mournes some of the granite peaks have shale 'caps'.

After the granite appears the flow of the river changes, with the descending waters forming a skin over flat pavements of rock, or hurrying noisily through gutters formed from faults or cracks. Another bridge is passed by on the way up, and soon you emerge out into the open alongside a forest of noble spruce. The Glen river flows out of a broad mountain-ringed valley; the river's former extent when it drained the last of the ice cap on this side of the Mournes can be guessed by looking at the height of and width between its ancient banks.

On the far side of the river the ruins of a conical-roofed icehouse stand; this insulated structure was used for the storage of collected ice in the wintertime, which was subsequently sold in blocks to Newcastle merchants and the big houses the following summer.

The path through heather and grass takes you high along the river's ancient banks; there are plenty of sheltered spots in the little valley beside the waters suitable for picnics. Soon after leaving the forestry behind, it is apparent that the path is coinciding with an older, stone-paved path, albeit recently refurbished and drained. Although I could find no reference to this in the Mourne literature, I assume that it might be an old pilgrim path to the summit of Donard, where St Domengard, or Dominic, is said to have had a hermitage.

Whatever the age or purpose of the paved path, it becomes very useful as you proceed. Nearly 90 minutes after setting out, the path takes you down to stepping stones across the river. This is the termination of this walk: find a dry spot and sit awhile before returning downhill. The views from here are marvellous: to the left is Slieve Commedagh rising above a little col called the Pot of Pulgarve; while the town of Newcastle is clear below, with the lagoon-like Dundrum Inner Bay beyond, and the waters of Strangford Lough beyond that again. If you wish to go further, see the next walk, 'The Glen River and Bloody Bridge River', below, otherwise return the way you came.

♦ WALK 15: THE GLEN RIVER AND BLOODY BRIDGE RIVER, CO. DOWN ♦

Here is a spectacular walk for more energetic and ambitious river walkers that requires a drop-off and pick-up at the end of the day, or two cars. The route follows the Glen river almost to its source and then climbs over the saddle between Slieve Donard and Slieve Commedagh to reach the source of the Bloody Bridge river and follows it as it, like the Mournes, sweeps down to the sea. The pick-up or second car should be arranged for the car park at Bloody Bridge, 3 km south of Newcastle on the coast road.

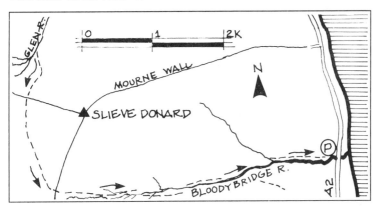

Walking time: Allow 5 hours
How to get there: As the Glen river.
Terrain: Between the Glen river and the saddle between Donard and Commedagh you negotiate rough stony mountain paths, quite steep in places initially. The descent beside the Bloody Bridge river is on rough stony tracks and paths through heather.
Map: NIOS Discoverer Series Sheet 29

Follow the indications given for the Glen river, and crossing the river by the stepping stones, continue to climb the old pathway. The plan now is to climb to and cross the saddle ahead to reach the source of the Bloody Bridge river. The climb is steep and you should take plenty of breaks to allow you to admire the vista opening up to the north; below you, the Glen river divides into a series of brooks and disappears into the bog.

Soon the incline levels out as the saddle is reached, and crossing in front of you is the Mourne Wall. This quite astonishing construction, a Great Wall of China in miniature, was built between 1909 and 1922 to define the catchment areas of the mountain reservoirs. The wall is about 1.5 m high and thick enough to walk on, and stretches an incredible 64 km over the Mournes, crossing fifteen summits. It can be difficult to understand how the wall ever got built at all when you realise that, although some of the stones used must weigh a ton and the logistics of getting workmen to the 'site' each day must have been horrendous, the wall can have had no actual physical effect on the catchment areas.

The highest summit in Ulster at 852 m, Slieve Donard, is 1 km away to the east and can be reached by following the wall up to the left; it is a very steep climb, but the views from the top, which in clear weather include the Isle of Man, are most rewarding.

To continue on to the Bloody Bridge river, cross the wall by the stone steps provided. A new vista now greets you; the marvellous rugged profiles of the south-east Mournes lie ahead, and beyond, the flat pasture-lands extending southwards towards the opening to Carlingford Lough.

Continue south for a short distance to reach a well-worn path called the Brandy Pad crossing east to west, and follow it to the left as it takes you to the Mourne Wall again on the shoulder between Slieve Donard and Chimney Rock mountain. The Brandy Pad is said to have been a smugglers' route from the coast to the hinterland in the 18th century, whereby wines, spirits, tobacco, tea and sugar would have been hauled to inland distribution centres such as Hilltown, which counted ten public houses in a village of twenty-one houses in the early 19th century.

On the eastern side of the wall another new view greets you; the Irish Sea stretches to the horizon framed by Chimney Rock mountain and the southern slopes of Donard. In between is the valley of the Bloody Bridge river; a vague winding path takes you downhill past a series of rivulets that have cut into the ground and trickle and gather to become one splashing brook.

After a while the stream is interrupted by a substantial granite quarry, where up until recently stone was extracted for paving and building. The water of the stream disappears into the rubble of the quarry and reappears on the slopes below. Stay on one of the faint paths on the left side of the river; there is a tempting roadway on the right bank, but it is mainly composed of loose cobbles and can be uncomfortable underfoot.

The path wends its way downhill crossing tributaries by stepping stones; at this level it is possible to see a series of overgrown roads rising up both sides of the valley to serve other disused quarries. Soon the river digs its way deep into boulder clay to form a ravine. The path improves as it descends through bracken and a stile is crossed just before another tributary joins from the left; near here is an ideal rocky pool in which to enjoy a bathe after a warm descent of the mountain.

Before reaching the main coast road the old and now disused stone-arched Bloody Bridge is passed; it is said a number of Newry Protestants were massacred here in the unhappy year of 1641, giving the place its name. The public road and car park, and the end of this walk, are a few metres further on.

THE GLENARIFF RIVER

The Glenariff river rises on the high Antrim Plateau and flows south and east to drop into one of the famous nine Glens of Antrim. I describe two contrasting walks on this river's short course to the sea, one that follows the tumultuous descent of the river into the glen, and the other that follows its peaceful course along the glen's flat floor.

♦ WALK 16: THE UPPER GLENARIFF RIVER, CO. ANTRIM ♦

This walk brings you along the upper reaches of the Glenariff river where it is punctuated by a series of spectacular waterfalls as it flows through Glenariff Forest Park. Timber walkways and staircases, originally built a hundred years ago when the place first became a tourist attraction, negotiate the more difficult ravines, and the humid jungle-like microclimate makes the place a botanist's delight. There is a small charge to enter the park, which does supply the facilities of a small restaurant, toilets and a little interpretative centre.

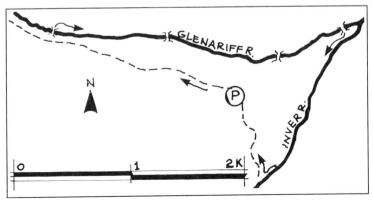

Walking time: 1 hour and 20 minutes round trip
Terrain: Forestry paths and timber walkways; the depth of the ravines necessitates steep descents and ascents by rustic staircases.
How to get there: Heading north on the Antrim coast road, pass through the village of Glenariff (or Waterfoot), and take the turn to the left signed for Glenariff Forest Park.
Map: NIOS Discoverer Series Sheets 5 and 9

There are four suggested trails in the park, marked with red, blue, yellow and white arrows; this walk combines two, the Waterfall Trail (blue arrows) and the Scenic Trail (red arrows). Set off from the map signboard in the car park following the blue arrows. A gravel track brings you along the steep side of a deep forested ravine which was carpeted with bluebells and ferns when I passed. Go left at the next fork in the path; at a clearing soon after, there is a magnificent view behind of the southernmost portal of Glenariff, beyond which in clear conditions the Mull of Galloway in Scotland lines the horizon.

After a few minutes the sound of the river hidden in a woodland of copper beech and oaks can be heard. The path ascends and descends teasingly until, going right at a junction, it descends deep into the ravine as the noise of crashing waters increases greatly. A bridge brings you over to the far side of the Glenariff river, a boisterous surging flood plunging over rocky cliffs, creating a damp world of bright green plants and dripping rock faces.

Elaborately constructed boardwalks cantilevered out over the river take you up and down along the ravine. The walls of the gorge are like a continuous rock garden hung down with exotic ferns, wild garlic, herb robert, borage and wild strawberry; the canopy of beech leaves overhead gives everything an eerie greenish hue. Seats are placed at strategic points along the route which allow you to relax and view the scene in comfort.

But for the path and walkways the place has a real sense of untamed jungle; no attempt has been made to tidy up fallen trees or debris swept down by winter floods, which over the years have taken on a coat of bright green moss and lichens.

After 20 minutes the path zig-zags down to the river level, and soon after, a graceful laminated timber bridge takes you to the far side again, and steeply uphill above another fine cascade. Yet a further descent of zig-zags is followed by a spiral down beside the tallest waterfall of the gorge, a spectacular 18 m cataract called the Tears of the Mountain.

The path shortly reaches an unexpected restaurant and bar where refreshments or even full meals are available. Beyond the restaurant the Glenariff is crossed again, and the path ascends beside a tributary, the Inver. A junction is reached where you depart from the blue arrow route and go straight to follow the red arrow route high up along the Inver. It too has its waterfalls and passes through a mixed forest of sycamores, larches and beeches; the quality of light in the wood changes with the species of tree.

Soon the path ascends very steeply through a sea of wild garlic and out into the open, to pass through a colourful shrubbery and arrive at the Visitors' Centre.

♦ WALK 17: THE LOWER GLENARIFF RIVER, CO. ANTRIM ♦

This is a peaceful rural walk along the tiny Glenariff river up one of Antrim's nine glens. Thackeray called this glen 'Switzerland in miniature', and it certainly has an Alpine flavour lent by the steep cliff-faced chalk and basalt mountains on each side, the erosion of which has provided the fertile soils of the flat, green valley between. The landscape is distinctive partly because farmland in the valley has been laid out in such a way as to give each farm an equal share of the fertile lowland, steep glenside and mountain land.

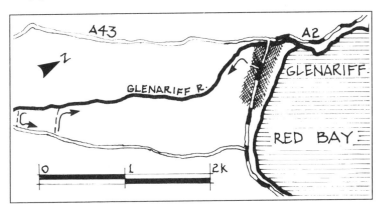

Walking time: 1 hour and 35 minutes there and back
Terrain: A grassy riverside pathway.
How to get there: Glenariff (or Waterfoot) village is on the Antrim coast road just south of Cushendall.
Maps: NIOS Discoverer Series Sheets 5 and 9

Park in the village and set out by turning right up the last street off the main street south of the river. Enter a little housing estate and cross diagonally over a green space on the right to a stile signed the Ulster Way. Cross the stile and follow a grassy path down to the slowly flowing Glenariff river. The path wends its way between the river and a herb-rich bank that was decorated by bluebells, herb robert, montbretia, dog roses and ferns when I passed. The river is narrow and quite shallow, and its man-made stone banks could be mistaken for those of a canal.

After a few minutes the village is left behind and the river is followed into the open countryside, with the gorse-speckled escarpments and Grand Canyon-like bluffs that form the walls of the glen rising on each side. Ten minutes after leaving the village a footbridge to the far side is passed and the river bends around to the right.

I saw more dippers in a short time on this river than any other; they use frequent limestone blocks that protrude above the water's surface as launching pads for their underwater forays. This is probably due to the consistently shallow, stone-covered bottom of the stream, scattered with gleaming shards of chalk, providing an excellent feeding habitat. Soon the gentle meandering of the river ceases and it goes straight as a canal up the glen. It was a clear day when I walked here, but looking back along the river as it straightened out I was surprised to be able to see the grey-blue slopes of the Scottish mountains across the North Channel.

Half an hour's walk beyond the village, at a concrete bridge over a tributary, the Ulster Way turns away from the riverbank; our route continues a little further along the bank although the grass is much longer now and the path less distinct. After nearly 10 minutes a field fence comes down to the water, but stiles will take you on further until a bridge is reached where you come to the extremity of this walk. Cross the last stile on to a laneway, turn left and make your way to the public road a short distance away, and turn left again.

Within 5 minutes the Ulster Way is met again; turn left yet again along a lane. A brook gurgles along beside the lane, its banks scattered with white cobbles of chalk containing nodules of flint. The river is soon reached and you can retrace your steps to the village.

◆ WALK 18: THE GLENEALO RIVER, GLENDALOUGH, CO. WICKLOW ◆

The Glenealo rises in the high moorland of the Wicklow Mountains and flows eastwards to cascade into the deep glacial valley of Glendalough and feed the two lakes of that famous place.

This walk is a foray into the fastness of the mountains, past the Upper Lake and up an old zig-zag track beside the cascading Glenealo to reach mineworkings that were abandoned nearly a hundred years ago. The views and surroundings all the way are magnificent; look out for peregrines that nest in the cliffs above the valley, deer that are often seen in herds of up to sixty animals, and feral goats with their shaggy coats and long curved horns.

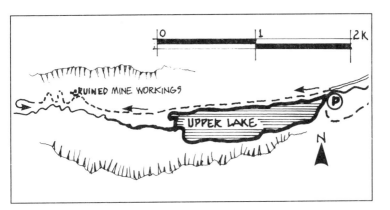

Walking time: 2½ hours; Climb: 300 m
Terrain: Half of this walk can be followed on a good gravel track, the rest on the remains of the old mine road, rugged in places, and riverside paths, some a little boggy.
How to get there: Glendalough is on the R757, 3 km west of Laragh, Co. Wicklow. When you reach the hotel in Glendalough, drive on to the Upper Lake car park.
Map: OS Discovery Series Sheet 56

Leave the car park following a shaded path beside the river towards the Upper Lake, and when the lake is reached after a few minutes, follow a pathway that winds through the Scots pines along its north shore. Above this pathway and parallel to it is a good forestry road, the old road to the mines; it can be used as an alternative route to the end of the lake. The lake fills a dramatic steep-sided glacial valley scoured out eons ago by a glacier. Originally the Lower and Upper Lakes were combined into one long lake, but the Poulanass river on the far side of the valley carried down millions of tons of sand and mud from the heights over the last 10,000 years and divided the lake into the two that exist today.

A few hundred metres along the lake shore search the cliff-face opposite for a rectangular cave about 10 m above the water level. This is the legendary St Kevin's Bed, which the saint is said to have lived in as a hermit 1,400 years ago. It was probably originally made by Bronze Age people to serve as a burial place.

The Upper Lake is up to 32 m deep and contains small trout and charr, a species common to deep mountain lakes. There are signs recommending no swimming at the eastern end of the lake, but I must say I have dipped in here on hot days; if you keep very close to the shore, you will not be out of your depth, but take care of submerged branches etc.

At the end of the wood the path rises to join the old road to the mines, which continues at a higher level along the lake side. Not far on, the western end of the lake is reached, where the Glenealo river meanders into it beside a picturesque crescent-shaped sandy beach. The dramatic upper end of the valley comes into view now, and you can see the zig-zag path that will take you up to this level.

Further along here, look out for signs in the cliffs on both sides for the interface between the granite that was pushed upwards as molten rock 400 million years ago, and the layered and the much older shiny schist that it burst through. The schist is a softer rock and therefore is clothed in heather, while the granite supports less foliage. Here, you may be fortunate to catch sight of a peregrine, for the rare birds nest in these inaccessible cliffs. Even if you do not see them, you may hear their plaintive squealing calls echoing across the valley as they soar high above.

The old road soon reaches the remains of the mine workings, which were first begun here about 1800 and ceased production in 1920. The actual adits or mine shafts can be identified by the cascades of light-coloured loose rock emanating from the cliffs up to the right. The light-coloured material is quartz in which galena, or lead ore, is found. If you find a heavy piece of quartz that has dark shadows in it, and break it open with a larger stone, you may reveal a silvery-blue jewel-like cube of galena.

Nearly 2,000 people were employed in these mines and their neighbours in the Glendasan valley to the north when lead prices were high before new, much richer African mines were discovered. The rock was crushed here and the ore extracted and brought by mule train to Wicklow to be shipped out to a smelter in Wales. The long-buried lead ores combined with deposits of arsenic and zinc now on the surface have prevented any but the most resilient lichens from thriving on the great piles of rock, and it will be centuries before these scars disappear.

Continue westwards through the ruins of the mine buildings as the road, much eroded in places, climbs towards the zig-zag track. Herds of feral goats can often be seen across the valley here; they are the descendants of domestic goats that escaped to the wild. As you ascend the zig-zag track there are opportunities to make your way over, with care, to where the Glenealo river cascades down into the valley, and there are a couple of shaded pools where you can have a refreshing dip on a hot day.

From the upper level of the valley, there is a marvellous view back to Glendalough. Meandering paths, some very boggy, will take you along the banks of the river as it flows over great flags of granite and cascades into shaded pools. There are many places along here that are safe for swimming if you take the usual precautions.

Further on, on the south side of the river, are more ruined buildings and heaps of crushed quartz. These mark the end of our walk; you can return the same way, or if you are still feeling energetic, you can follow the river westwards a while longer into a remote moorland wilderness.

♦ WALK 19: THE GLENSHELANE RIVER, CO. WATERFORD ♦

The Glenshelane river rises in the eastern Knockmealdown Mountains and flows southwards out of a deep and remote wooded valley to reach the Blackwater near Cappoquin. This walk takes you along the river up into that valley, and back by the public road.

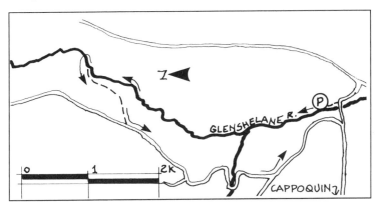

Walking time: 2 hours and 40 minutes
Terrain: Forestry roads and tarmac.
How to get there: Take the R669 eastwards out of Cappoquin; go right at a junction 800 m beyond the town, cross a bridge and turn left into a car park beside the river.
Maps: OS Discovery Series Sheet 74; Half-inch Sheet 22

Follow a grassy riverside pathway away from the car park and upstream which after a few minutes joins a narrow forestry track. The track climbs the steep side of Glenshelane through a pleasant informal forest of beech, oak and scrub, leaving the river far below for a while. Descending again, a footbridge to the other side of the river (which leads across to the dirt road running to the scout camping ground in Walk Number 26) is passed by before the track continues to ascend and descend, becoming more grass covered and more pleasant to walk on the further up the glen it penetrates.

After about 15 minutes, near a clearing, a meeting of waters is reached where the combined Monavugga and Glenfallia rivers join the Glenshelane. On higher ground a fine white-painted, bow-gabled cottage overlooks the meeting of the rivers.

Follow the Glenshelane upstream as it cascades down through a dark, fern- and rhododendron-shrouded rocky gorge. When I walked here the track for a short distance had been recently swept away by a landslide. Near by I found a glorious clump of pale pink foxgloves, a variety not nearly as common as the purple-flowered one. Further on there was an avenue, a dense margin of the more common foxgloves, taking their turn to display purple after the last of the rhododendrons overhanging them had faded.

Soon the rushing of the river recedes again below in a jungle of scrub as the track climbs into the open. Knocknanask, one of the many summits of the Knockmealdown Mountains, comes into sight over the trees ahead, beyond pinnacled Crow Hill. The steep far side of the glen is a dense mass of deciduous trees making a wonderful texturous backdrop to the scene.

About an hour after setting out, an area is reached where the coniferous trees have been harvested in recent years. Stripped of the densely packed foliage cover, the glen takes on a real grandeur, the steepness of its sweeping flanks accentuated by the lines of old preserved oak trees following each stream that descends into the Glenshelane river. It was here that I spotted a small herd of deer high up on the glenside, just as they spotted me. There were about six of them, and they all turned their heads towards me, their ears raised like antennae. Then, with a high-pitched call, they turned, and with their brilliant white rumps bouncing up and down, ran into the cover of a copse of oak, disturbing a raucously protesting pair of blue jays.

The steep-sided glen swings left and right as it follows the course of the meandering river; soon after a forestry track comes into view on the far side of the river; watch out carefully for a footbridge at a clearing. This is the turning point of the walk; you will have gone too far if the track you are following turns right and heads away from the river before petering out.

Take the time to sit awhile on the bridge in the shade of the hazelnut tree, swinging your legs over the dark waters, and enjoy the peace of this remote place.

To return, cross the bridge and, turning left, follow the forestry track, going right at a fork a few minutes later. The track climbs high, giving you a very good impression of the depth and width of Glenshelane before levelling out and turning west to reach the public road at the townland of Lyre East. The road meanders south and enters forestry again shortly before crossing the Lyre bridge (see Walk Number 26).

Turn left at the main Mount Mellery road, and again left at the next junction to bring you back to the starting point.

♦ WALK 20: THE GWEEBARRA RIVER, CO. DONEGAL ♦

The Gweebarra river, the remains of an ancient glacial river, flows out of Lough Barra, south of the Derryveagh mountains, and maintains a course that is almost precisely south-west, broadening dramatically before it reaches the sea by the sweeping sands of Gweebarra Bay. It is a beautiful river of great contrasts; this short stroll, best taken in the early morning or late evening, brings you along a quiet inland stretch known only to salmon anglers, herons and otters. Legend tells us the river was created when the land opened up to allow St Conall, swimming frantically, to escape a sea monster he encountered in Gweebarra Bay.

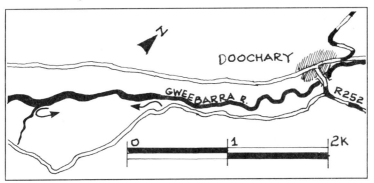

Walking time: 45 minutes there and back
Terrain: Grassy riverbank, eroding in places, boggy in others.
How to get there: The village of Doochary is on the R252, about 12 km east of Dungloe.
Map: OS Discovery Series Sheet 11

Cross the bridge eastwards out of Doochary and turn immediately right on to a side road. After about 1.5 km, when the road comes to within a few metres of the river beside where a great sheet of bedrock bursts out of the ground, park opposite a narrow opening in the roadside fence. Descend to the riverbank and head downriver.

The Gweebarra here is tidal, and alternates between the quiet of a meandering stream between broad sandbanks and a vigorous, fast-flowing water course. On the opposite side of the river there is a place of ancient pilgrimage where a *turas* or 'pattern' is held to commemorate St Conall on 15 August each year. Pilgrims pray as they circle a small cairn and two stones that are said to have the shapes of the saint's elbows and knees in them, made when he crawled ashore after being chased by the sea monster.

The grassy banks of the river are well cropped by sheep and make for comfortable walking initially. The rugged mountains to the east send outcrops of bare sandstone down into the valley almost to the banks of the river, amongst which the ruins of stone-built cottages hide, hardly discernible from the natural geology. The waters of the river, slowly moving and patterned with concentric rings made by jumping fish when I passed, are stained by the peat of the hills to a Guinness colour.

After heavy rain the waters of the Gweebarra river can rise dramatically as the naked rock of the mountains to the north sheds the rainfall; detritus of seaweed and straw woven into the wire of the riverside fences indicates the level to which the river can rise. In places you have to walk inside the fence as the riverbank has eroded.

As a whitewashed, tin-roofed cottage higher up the hill is passed, the terrain becomes a little rough in places. The river soon broadens out and the rounded Derkbeg Hill comes into view ahead. The far bank, sloping steeply up from the water, is overhung by a grove of oak trees, the remains of what was probably once a more dense oak forest, recalled in the local townland names of Derryhenny, meaning the oak grove of the cultivated field, and Glenaltaderry, meaning the valley of the high oaks.

About 20 minutes after setting out, a strong-flowing tributary is reached, flowing down from Croaghleheen, that nearby rounded sandstone hill. There is a grassy bank here where you can sit and take in the peaceful surroundings, and if you are as fortunate as I was when I did so, you may see an otter. He came down the tributary, swimming along the far bank, foraging, diving and surfacing, and when he reached the bank opposite me, he looked across curiously. His approach had given me the time to get my camera ready, and he was not put out by the whirr of the mechanism as I took shot after shot. He even started to swim over towards me, when he suddenly took fright and dived, leaving a trail of bubbles on the water's surface marking his course back to the sanctuary of the overhung far bank.

♦ WALK 21: THE KILBRONEY RIVER, THE FAIRY GLEN, ROSTREVOR, CO. DOWN ♦

The Kilbroney river, also known as the Rostrevor river, flows down from the steep escarpment that forms the western boundary of the Mourne Mountains and empties into Carlingford Lough at the beautiful village of Rostrevor. The walk described is a wonderful short stroll along the river in the magical woodland of Kilbroney Park.

Walking time: 30 minutes there and back
Terrain: Good woodland paths.
How to get there: The walk starts on the eastern side of Rostrevor at Kilbroney bridge. Rostrevor is 3 km east of Warrenpoint on the A2 Kilkeel road.
Map: NIOS Discoverer Series Sheet 29

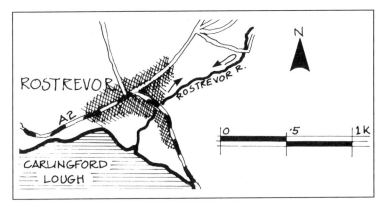

Rostrevor is a gem of a village, and the entrance to the Fairy Glen is overlooked by an informal but elegant cluster of modest Georgian houses with delicate fanlights and ivy-covered cottages with diamond-paned windows. Go through a gate and follow the east bank of the rushing stream as it descends towards the lough through a leafy tunnel of beeches. There are many tiny cascades along the way in this birdsong-loud woodland as you ascend gently towards the steep wooded hills that rise above Rostrevor.

The Fairy Glen and the Fairy Hill beyond are said to be the home of the 'brooneys', a species of fairy known for their love of practical jokes, and if you listen hard enough you may hear in the splashing and rushing of the river their tinkling laughter.

There is a mixture of beech, sycamore and holly trees interspersed with tall and ancient oaks of great girth. Just before you cross over the first little green-railed footbridge, see if you can spot, on the far bank of the river, a boundary hedge guarded by contorted ash trees that look like a couple of surreal animals.

The river becomes more vigorous as you ascend the path, fighting its way downhill over exposed sheets of rock and past scattered moss-covered boulders. Some of the trees along the river's edge have gnarled trunks that seem to grow directly from the bedrock, the wood and the stone appearing to merge into one.

Abruptly the woodland comes to an end at a bridge. From here you can return to the centre of the village, or, if you have developed a taste for the place, you can retrace your steps a few metres and turn left up a path that follows the course of a babbling brook east and uphill through the wood. There are many options to follow, including seeking out the Rostrevor Oakwoods National Nature Reserve, 17 acres of mature sessile oakwood, or climbing to the cairn on the top of Slieve Martin, 485 m above sea level. An alternative would be to walk out the Hilltown road about 1 km to the ruin of Cill Brónach, which gives the river its name, where you will find a holy well and the grave of Paddy Murphy, 1834–1862, who was at one time the tallest man in the world!

♦ WALK 22: KILLARY HARBOUR, CO. GALWAY ♦

Killary Harbour is Ireland's only true fiord, collecting a number of rivers such as the Erriff, the Bunowen and the Bundorragh, and delivering them to the Atlantic Ocean.

I describe an exhilarating walk along the edge of the fiord, overlooked by the great bulk of Connaught's highest mountain, Mweelrea. For those who want a longer walk, a return loop is suggested that passes through a typical slice of Connemara, with its rocky shores, lakes and mountains.

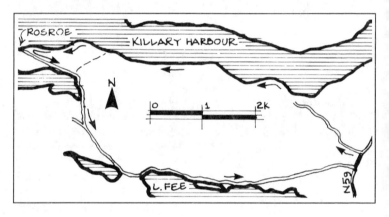

Walking time:
Option A: To Rosroe and back along Killary, 4 hours there and back
Option B: To Rosroe and back by Little Killary Bay and Lough Fee, 4½ hours
Terrain:
Option A: Track/green road, very wet at times, and a little rough for a short distance, but very comfortable going generally. Suitable for all.
Option B: As above, plus tarmac public road.
How to get there: The walk starts where a side road joins the N59, 7 km west of Leenaun, Co. Mayo, a couple of hundred metres west of Tullyconor bridge.
Maps: OS Discovery Series Sheet 37; Tim Robinson's (Folding Landscapes) Connemara 1-inch map

Follow the narrow tarmac road, bounded by rhododendrons and willows, as it twists and winds downhill towards the waters of Killary. Soon a little beach backed by trees is seen below; nestling in the trees is Derrynasliggaun Lodge, owned by the Killary Adventure Centre, which was a Republican prisoner-of-war camp during the Civil War.

Ahead, the deep coombs and sensuous curves of Mweelrea rise like a wall on the far side of Killary, and looking back towards Leenaun, the mass of mountains sweeping into the harbour is dominated by the flat-topped plateau of Devil's Mother.

Soon the tarmac runs out and more comfortable gravel and grass takes its place. The geology all around is spectacular, from the bulbous pink-hued, lichen-dappled hummocks of sandstone that project up through the peat bogs, to the immensity of Mweelrea's bulk across the harbour, the scale of which can be realised only when you see a fishing vessel close to the far shore.

Nearly an hour after setting out, as the track descends towards the shore, fences are left behind and their place is taken by scattered mountain ash, holly and the ubiquitous alder. The grassy surface is speckled all the way by yellow stars of tormentil, while damp patches beside the track sport sundew and butterwort in some abundance. The full extent of Killary out to the Atlantic Ocean is in sight now. The 13 fathom-deep inlet, formed by the action of ice during the glacial period, is Ireland's only fiord, and is said to have provided safe haven for the entire British fleet in times gone by.

The barely discernible undulations of old cultivation ridges, and the sad ruins of a stone-walled cottage passed on the left, are the only signs left of the substantial population that inhabited this area before the Great Famine. The track you walk on, however, is a most substantial construction which I thought had a military background, but an old man in Rosroe told me it had been built to provide employment during the famine.

Soon the grassy track leads you into the hamlet of Foher, passing the remains of a cottage flanked by thick rhododendron groves. One cottage above the track looks as though it has only recently become vacant; up behind it can be found a holy well dedicated to St Joseph, which local people told me provides cures for eye ailments.

After leaving the ruined hamlet the track is narrowed down by swathes of bracken; the power lines coming over the hill up to the left coincide with a rough path through cliff-sided Salrock Pass, said to have been formed by the devil attempting to drag the local saint, St Roc, away on the end of a chain. The rocky summit west of the pass extends out to the harbour as if to block your passage, but a stile over a wall leads on to a stony continuation of the track around the promontory.

The open sea comes into sight soon after, with a beacon tower identifying Inis Bearna across the narrow opening of the harbour. When you see the colourful fish farm floats of the Killary Salmon Company stretching out from the land, you know you are near Rosroe.

The landscape becomes more bare of soil and vegetation as you proceed, and the track less discernible. Reaching a stone wall, follow it westwards as it winds down past a cottage to reach the hamlet of Rosroe. Turn right to reach the harbour, overlooked by an An Óige hostel, which in its previous existence provided hospitality for the philosopher Wittgenstein, the poet Richard Murphy and the painter Paul Henry.

This is the end of Option A; after a suitable rest you can retrace your steps back down Killary to where you started out. If you are following Option B, leave the pier behind and follow the road up through the little hamlet; to the right the rocky bulk of Benchoona fills the horizon. After a few minutes the waters of Little Killary Bay come into view below, often scattered with colourful sailboards piloted by young people enjoying a stay at the Killary Adventure Centre. Like much of Connemara, the surrounds are a mixture of rugged, treeless, rock-scattered bogland, with frequent oasis-like and contrasting copses of luxuriant trees and shrubs. One such little enclave can be seen across the other side of the bay, clustered around Salrock House, built in 1836 by a Colonel Thomson who ran a Connemara estate of 8,000 acres.

As the road turns sharply to the right to pass along the eastern shore of the bay, note the overhead power lines going steeply uphill beside a rocky escarpment. If you have changed your mind and want to reduce your journey back to the start, follow the power lines up a rough path and over to the other side of the peninsula, to rejoin the track taken on the outward journey near Foher.

I cannot help feeling that the upturned curraghs that lay on the shore when I walked here are a sight that will soon become very rare; there seems to have been an increase of fibreglass-hulled fishing boats over recent years at the expense of the old traditional workhorse.

On the far side of the bay the road climbs between thick hedges of fuchsia which were blazing red when I passed, backed in one place by a field full of flame-coloured montbretia. I do not know what the ecological effects of these two imported species are in Connemara, but the place would be a lot less colourful without them.

The road takes you high above the valley and then down into the next, where Lough Muck lies below steep-sided Benchoona. Bear left at the road junction, noting the remains of ancient cultivation ridges and much-eroded rocky field walls rising up the slopes on the far side of the lake.

The rushing river that flows into Lough Muck is followed around a corner to reach Lough Fee, extending silver into the distance, backed by the dark Maumturk Mountains. The road takes you on a grand promenade along the shore of this broad expanse of water, passing the heavily wooded Illaunroe. Sir William Wilde, a great lover of Connemara, built a fishing lodge here in 1853, to which his son Oscar came for holidays during the 1870s.

Leaving the lake behind, the road takes you out on to a bleak moorland with the Maumturks looming ever more massive ahead. About 12 hours after leaving Rosroe you should reach the main road (N59). Turn left for 400 m to reach your starting point.

◆ WALK 23: THE RIVER LEE AT GOUGANE BARRA, CO. CORK ◆

The River Lee rises in the old red sandstone mountains above Com Rua at the head of a wonderful glacial coomb called Gougane Barra, where St Finbar founded an island hermitage in the 6th century. Nothing remains of the original foundation, but a memorial church stands beside an older ruin where pilgrims make their rounds of the stations on the last Sunday of September every year. The planting of a forest of Sitka spruce, Douglas fir and larch has hidden some of the beauty of the valley, and Coillte charge a £1 per person entrance fee, but they have laid out a number of family walks to try to make up for it. The walk described uses parts of these to take you up the head of the valley close to the source of the River Lee.

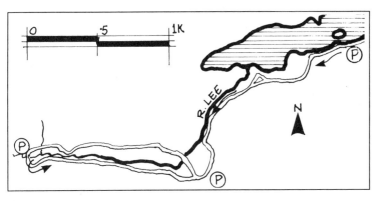

Walking time: 1¾ hours there and back
Terrain: Tarmac road and forest paths.
How to get there: Gougane Barra is 6 km west of Ballingeary village, on the R584 to Bantry, Co. Cork.
Map: OS Discovery Series Sheet 85

Leave Cronin's bar which overlooks Gougane Barra Lake and walk up the road beside the water. Near by, the little rhododendron-cocooned church dedicated to St Finbar, who is said to have founded a hermitage on the little island in the 6th century, is very photogenic in its lake setting, with the high mountain escarpment forming a spectacular background. The local graveyard is passed on the left, and shortly after, the most amazing public toilet you are ever likely to see, a Silver Award winner in the Superloo of Ireland competition!

Rounding a corner, the rocky cliffs that form the end of the great glacial coomb where the River Lee rises come into view. The road takes you away from the lake and brings you to the entrance of the Coillte Park, where £1 per person has to be paid (a fee that strangely applies equally to persons on foot or in a car).

Continue along the road looking out for a little stream in the trees to the right; this is the infant River Lee. When you see a footbridge across the stream, leave the road and cross over. The Lee was glass-like when I passed here, the water imperceptibly flowing along a regular-sided course like a tiny canal. The bottom was sandy with frequent deep, clear pools, where fish darted and splashed. A grey wagtail bounced, bobbed and skipped along the bank, chirping all the way.

Carry on along the path beside the river until it comes out of the trees, and follow it away from the river briefly, through a cathedral of spruce trees, to reach the road again at a stone-built public toilet. Follow the road to a gravel track which takes you back, out of the trees again, to join the Lee after a few minutes.

Cross a timber bridge to the far side; take care underfoot, as the tree roots can trip you easily. As the stream moves away from the road and bears around to the left, look out for a slab of sandstone bedrock with ripple marks like those the sea makes on a sandy beach; these ripples have been frozen in time for over 300 million years.

The coomb becomes narrower the further west you go, and through the trees you can see towering cliffs of old red sandstone on each side. The waters of the Lee are descending the steeper ground now over a series of small cascades. The stream bed is littered with great grass-thatched blocks of stone, washed down by the Lee millennia ago when it was a much more powerful water course, fuelled by a melting ice cap high in the mountains.

After a final steep climb up some steps and across a couple of footbridges, the gorge narrows and the Lee is reduced to a series of cascades descending vertically from the tree-shaded cliffs above, marking the end of this walk. You may return by the way you came or by the tarmac road, which is reached by a flight of rustic steps.

THE RIVER LIFFEY

James Joyce wrote in *Finnegans Wake* that the Liffey begins 'on the spur of the hill in old Kippure, in birdsong and shearing time, but first of all, worst of all, the wiggly livvly, she sideslipped out by a gap . . . while Sally her nurse was sound asleep . . .' The river rises near the Sally Gap just south of the Dublin/Wicklow border, and commences a roundabout 138 km journey to Dublin Bay. Passing through County Wicklow it swells to become the main reservoir for Dublin. In County Kildare, it graces the towns of Kilcullen, Newbridge, Celbridge, Leixlip and Lucan before it offers itself to Ireland's capital and flows into the Irish Sea. I describe two walks along the Liffey, one close to where the river rises, and the other where it exits from the great reservoir lakes at Blessington in County Wicklow.

♦ WALK 24: THE RIVER LIFFEY AT THE CORONATION PLANTATION, CO. WICKLOW ♦

The first kilometres of the Liffey's course bring it through the unique uplands of the Coronation plantation, the remains of an 1831 forest plantation which was never completed. The Wicklow and Dublin Mountains usually consist of either open expanses of treeless moorland or thick coniferous forests; the Coronation plantation is today a wonderful mixture of the two, a moor with a broad and picturesque scatter of pines, oaks, alders and rowan, which accompany the River Liffey westwards. The walk described below follows the Liffey to the sandpits at Ballysmuttan, and returns taking you on a diversion up the Lugnalee tributary into remote and open moors below Gravale mountain.

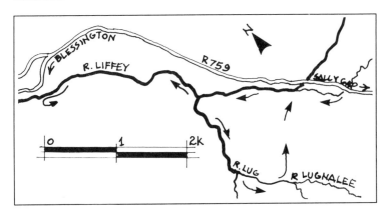

Walking time: Allow 4 hours
Terrain: Rough riverbank paths for most of the way, but a few short scrambles and a few very boggy patches. If you follow the Lugnalee towards its source you will be crossing open, pathless and often rough moorland, as you will when you return to the Liffey over the hill; be sure this part of the route is not attempted if visibility is bad.
How to get there: The Sally Gap is a crossroads on the R115, 26 km south of Dublin.
Map: OS Discovery Series Sheet 56

About 2 km west of the Sally Gap on the Blessington road, at the first little copse of trees for many kilometres, where an unnamed brook passes under the road, the walk starts. Follow the brook along the right bank as it gurgles golden brown over granite boulders and meanders across the moor and away from the road. You can expect to see grey wagtails and dippers here, as well as snipe, meadow pipits, stonechats and red grouse. In summertime bursts of yellow broom hang over the water at regular intervals, as if planted deliberately. Within a short time, although the road is not far away, there is a sense of a remote wilderness, with the only human intervention the two TV masts on bare Kippure 3 km away to the north.

As the ground to the south begins to rise and the first conifers of the Coronation plantation are in sight, cross to the south side of the brook before it joins the young River Liffey, a more substantial stream coming from the north. Continue along the Liffey now on a rough path that ascends and descends the steep-sided south bank. Where there are boggy parts, or where the banks are too steep, climb uphill through bracken as far as necessary to avoid them.

The oaks, conifers and rowan trees become more frequent as you progress westwards, and the carpets of bluebells that extended well beyond them when I walked here were evidence that this was once a much-wooded place. You will sometimes hear a thundering sound as you walk; it is an echo that comes from the firing ranges at Kilbride rolling across the mountains.

About 45 minutes after setting out, a couple of stone-built ruins come into sight up on the far hillside. The first is all that remains of the Shanamuck Iron Mines, worked here in the 18th century. The second, a fine Victorian high-gabled house, still partially roofed, was built in association with the Coronation plantation in the 1830s, and was lived in until the 1980s. A track leading down from this last ruin crosses the Liffey by way of a concrete bridge, after which the Liffey is joined by the Lugnalee stream, coming from a broad valley stretching south.

Cross the Lugnalee by stepping stones and continue along a path on the south bank of the Liffey under the dappled shade of mixed pines and oak between cushions of fraughans and bracken. Five minutes beyond the bridge there is a long grassy-banked pool-like section where trout leap, and where I have enjoyed a cooling swim in summertime.

Cross another tiny tributary from the south as it gurgles through a mossy glade; as before, take to the higher ground as the banks become boggy in places. About 15 minutes after crossing the Lugnalee you draw level with the beginning of a modern coniferous wood on the far side of the river, and soon after the ruins of Kippure House and its walled gardens can be seen up on the hill beyond it. The western boundary of the Coronation plantation lies across the river from the ruins, where the land becomes quite boggy; you may need to head for higher ground again to bypass this section. Further on the riverside trees dwindle and the rounded shape of bare Sorrell Hill comes into view with forested Ballynatona stretching north from it.

Soon another spur of high ground reaches north to the riverbank; two dormer windows in a slated roof peer over its summit. To the north the naked scree-sided Seefin looms above the forest. Marsh forget-me-nots speckle the boggy ground and green, blue and black damselflies flit along the water's edge.

About 90 minutes after setting out, you should see the riverbank dwindle ahead and give way to a low cliff of granite; here the walk terminates. In winter, with high run-off, it would be well to turn back at this point, but in summertime you can make your way a little further along the rocks to find a good spot for a picnic where the river cascades and flows over pavements of granite and forms pools deep enough to swim in.

Return the way you came until you cross the Lugnalee again. This time follow the Lugnalee upstream on the east bank under a canopy of oaks and Scots pines, and after a couple of minutes when the bank becomes steep and the river takes a sharp sweep around to the right, climb away from it south-east towards the higher ground, where you can see a stone pinnacle; a path through the bracken and heather will take you to it in a few minutes. It is an obelisk erected by the Marquess of Downshire to commemorate the development of the Coronation plantation, so called because it celebrated the coronation of the sailor king, William IV, in 1831. The inscriptions can be difficult to read but indicate that the trees were planted 'for a future supply of useful timber for the Estate and the improvement of the County and the Benefit of the Labouring Classes'.

Leaving the monument, head west 100 m or so through bracken to rejoin the riverbank, and follow it past copses of oaks and pines and the gnarled remains of many fallen trees. It is a great pity that this woodland is not regenerating itself, probably due to deer and sheep eating the seedlings; at the beginning of the 20th century the wood extended right across the valley; within fifty years it will probably be gone.

You have a choice as you proceed to walk along the riverbank or on the hillside high above it; the latter course will give you a fine view over the terrain and allow you to spot more wildlife. When I passed here I disturbed a stag, which sprang comically but disdainfully away to cover.

The river valley wends its way south into a vast amphitheatre of moorland under Gravale Hill and Duff Hill. About 20 minutes after leaving the Liffey behind, the pine trees peter out. When they do, cross on to the far bank of the Lugnalee and continue along it on the heathery banks as it bears around left. Where it divides again, follow the stream going left towards one lone Scots pine which has survived in the open moorland; this marks the place where you leave the stream behind. The terrain can be fairly rough here, and wet in wintertime, but there are always sheep tracks that wend their way over the driest ground. When you draw level with the lonesome pine, you have a choice; I found that the terrain gets very boggy the further upstream you proceed, but if you wish to explore further, you may ascend the stream into the hills to where it rises in Carriglaur. Otherwise, cross the river and head uphill towards the pine, and take a rest in its shelter or shade to soak in the panorama laid out at your feet.

You must now head directly uphill over open moorland away from the tree; within minutes the masted summit of Kippure comes into view ahead. Head towards it over the hill and down the other side until you eventually reconnect with the Liffey, which you should do within about 45 minutes. Turn right and follow it back to your starting point.

♦ WALK 25: THE RIVER LIFFEY AT THE BLESSINGTON LAKES, CO. WICKLOW ♦

This is a 30 minute stroll, full of history ancient and modern, starting at a 14th-century tower house and touching on the River Liffey and the Blessington Reservoir before returning to the castle. The faint paths through tall grasses give a real, if short, wilderness feel; you could be in similar surroundings hunting for tigers in India! In wintertime this is a good route for spotting pheasant, snipe, herons, Bewick swans, lapwings, teal and curlews. A large flock of greylag geese, the ancestor of the domestic goose, flies from Iceland to winter here each year.

Walking time: 30 minutes
Terrain: Old boreen and rough riverside paths; can be mucky in wet weather.
How to get there: Take the N81 south out of Dublin to the village of Blessington; take the left turn off the main street after the church and keep on straight along the northern shore of the lake for 3 km. As the road bears around in a long curve to the right, look out for a small castle to the right of the road. There is parking in an adjacent picnic area.
Map: OS Discovery Series Sheet 56

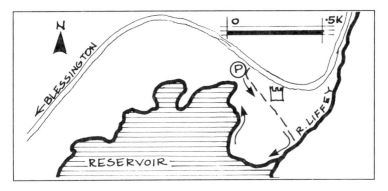

Take the track leading towards the lake; after a short distance it intersects an old, grass-grown road lined with ash, elder and hawthorn, which became disused when the lakes were created in 1940; turn left and follow it for less than 10 minutes, passing through a larch plantation, and reach the banks of the young River Liffey. There is a ford here which was in use into this century, and would have been the reason for the castle being sited here originally.

Turn right along a faint path through the grass along the bank, or if the water level is low, you can walk safely for a time on the sandy shore. The grasses here are related to the bamboo, and after a while, particularly for small children, it can be like tracking through the African bush. The northernmost edge of the Blessington Lakes are met after a few minutes. The lakes are man-made and involved drowning part of the valley of the Liffey and the construction of a dam at Poulaphuca between 1938 and 1940. Seventy-six homesteads had to be vacated, the owners compensated, and burials in Burgage cemetery moved to higher ground during the process. Local tradition says that on certain days you can see buildings beneath the water, but in fact today only the shapes of old ditches and the stumps of trees on the lake bed, visible when the water level is low, remain of what was there before.

In wintertime the lake here is a great place to watch birds. Snipe and pheasant are plentiful along the margins, while lapwing, teal, curlews and greylag geese can be seen in large numbers. If the water level is low, look out for a row of tree stumps which were a field boundary before 1940. You will also see many shells of surprisingly big freshwater otter-clams, fished up and eaten by geese.

The paths through the long grass may be faint at times, but keep gently bearing around to the right to follow a sometimes dried-up inlet back to the castle, which you can keep in sight the whole way.

The castle is the sole survivor of three that originally stood in this area, from which the townland gets the name Three Castles. It was about 200 years old when there was a battle here between the English and their Irish allies, the O'Tooles, against the Fitzgeralds, during which part of the building was destroyed by fire. You can see the remains of the thick walls of the destroyed section and the shape of its outline in the grass. The stones of the ruined section, as was common in Ireland, represented a handy and economic quarry, and probably eventually went to build many houses in the neighbourhood. The farmhouse across the road may have been one of them; in its gable it displays the stones of a decorative cut-granite window hundreds of years older than the house

♦ WALK 26: THE MONAVUGGA RIVER, CAPPOQUIN, CO. WATERFORD ♦

The Monavugga river rises on the southern slopes of Knockfallia, one of the many summits of the Knockmealdown Mountains, and flows south to reach the Blackwater River near Cappoquin.

This woodland river walk ends at a holy well in a rocky place where the Virgin Mary is said to have appeared in 1985, and which has since become a place of devout pilgrimage, indicating that the mystical powers of springs imbued by the ancients is not necessarily a thing of the past.

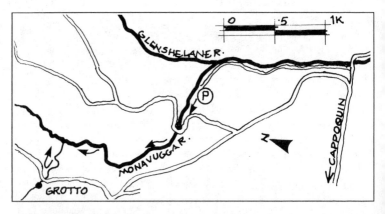

Walking time: 1 hour and 20 minutes
Terrain: Comfortable forestry roads.
How to get there: Take the R669 eastwards out of Cappoquin; go right at a junction 800 m beyond the town and almost immediately turn in left on to a gravel road. Four km from Cappoquin, the starting point, a scout camping ground, is reached.
Maps: OS Discovery Series Sheet 74; OS Half-inch Sheet 22

Park near the scout camping ground; the road beyond here serves a dwelling house and is private. Follow an avenue of poplars through the camping ground on to a pathway; the Monavugga flows darkly over to the right. The forest is a damp green place of rhododendrons, hollies and oaks, the ground and much of the lower parts of the trees richly clothed in mosses.

After a few minutes the tall Lyre bridge (I thought the name had musical connotations, but find that the word is the Gaelic term for a river fork) is reached which takes the public road over the river ravine. A timber walkway takes you to the other side of the bridge, and then a footbridge is crossed on to the far bank.

This is a very pleasant and cool place to walk in summertime. Not many plant species thrive in the subdued light that leaks in through the canopy of conifers, but you will find an abundance of ferns of different varieties, and in late summer and autumn a range of fungi enjoys the dim light, dampness and shelter. One such fungus you will be aware of, even if you do not see it. The name of the stinkhorn sums up its most memorable feature; it produces a strong, unpleasant sickly sweet smell to attract flies which feed on its spores and, in turn, distribute them.

The river's course is scattered with great sandstone boulders polished and shaped by eons of rushing mountain waters; many of them sport a lush thatch of ferns and mosses.

After about 10 minutes a stile is crossed into the open, dramatically bright after the gloom of the forest. The coniferous forest continues as a great bank of trees on the far side of the river as the path you follow wends its way through a grassy area, passing a pleasant little stony beach of colourful pebbles of sandstone, quartz and limestone.

Further on another footbridge takes you across to the far bank again and uphill into a spruce forest, briefly away from the river which glints through the trees below. The riverside is rejoined at a place where its waters cascade noisily over a tumbled confusion of boulders. A little further on a tributary joins the main stream through a moss-covered sinuous and narrow ravine in the sandstone bedrock to create a most picturesque meeting-of-the-waters.

Yet another bridge takes you across the river again, and the pathway goes steeply uphill to where a stile brings you out into the open and on to a forestry road. The river can still be heard as it rushes along far below; follow the road past a beautifully restored old forge to reach the public road. Turn left and cross Mellery bridge to reach the end of this walk at a Marian shrine, a series of railway sleeper corrals and loggias gathered around a statue of the Virgin perched on a tree-shaded mossy cliff. The place is decorated with plants and shrubs, and at the back of the covered seating areas there is an array of objects of devotion such as crucifixes, pictures of the Sacred Heart and old plaster statues brought as gifts by pilgrims. The Virgin Mary is said to have appeared here to local people in August 1985. The shrine is rarely without at least a few people reciting the Rosary, and it is a place that will not fail to be thought provoking.

Just north of the shrine are the lands of Mount Mellery Abbey, founded by Irish Cistercians who had been expelled from France in 1832. What was once a remote and barren mountainside was, within ten years of their arrival, turned into a productive farm. There are not many monks left now, but the monastery still operates the tradition of offering accommodation to travellers free of charge.

THE RIVER NORE

The Nore, with the Suir and Barrow, is one of the Three Sisters rivers which drain most of the south-east of Ireland, and then unite to flow into Waterford Harbour in one broad stream. It rises in north Tipperary, not very far from where the Barrow rises, but takes a different route for 133 km, flowing through Kilkenny city, Thomastown and Inistioge before it finally meets the Barrow above New Ross. I describe two walks on the Nore, both originating in picturesque Thomastown.

♦ WALK 27: THE RIVER NORE, UPSTREAM FROM THOMASTOWN, CO. KILKENNY ♦

This walk is an introduction to the River Nore, taking you upstream past the old mills and rushing millraces of Thomastown, under a great railway viaduct and on to the boundary of Mount Juliet's famous golf course. Thomastown, founded by the Norman Thomas Fitz Anthony around A.D. 1200, combines an old-world atmosphere of narrow streets and well-preserved street fronts with good shops, pubs and restaurants. At the end of the main street there is the unusual sight of a 19th-century church built within the remains of a 13th-century church, and one of the buildings in Low Street, a bed and breakfast establishment, is a medieval tower house, complete with narrow stone-lined windows.

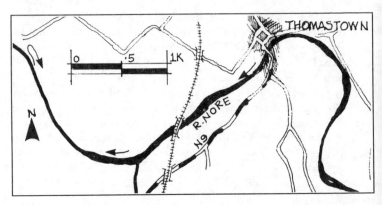

Walking time: Nearly 2 hours there and back
Terrain: Comfortable anglers' riverside paths with stiles and gates at fences, although the grass can be long and very wet after rain; suitable for all.
How to get there: Thomastown is on the R700, 18 km south-east of Kilkenny.
Map: OS Half-inch Sheet 19

Descend to the west side of the river at the 18th-century Thomastown bridge, following a sign that says 'Riverside Walk'. A path takes you past Mullins Castle, one of the original fourteen castles that reinforced the walled town and protected the original timber bridge built about 1346. A stile takes you on to the grassy riverbank beside the broad, strong-flowing Nore. On the far side of the river are two of the great corn mills that gave Thomastown its prosperity; there were twelve watermills in the area originally. The millraces are still running, one of them with sufficient force to drive a great wheel. The second large mill on the far bank is today used to house a school of art. The fine houses beyond the mills probably belonged to the millowners.

In a few minutes the grassy path takes you along the outlet of another millrace which used to drive a wheel at the mill building ahead. Bypass this building using stiles which again leave you out into a grassy pasture beside the great V-shaped weir that divides the river in three.

Above the weir the river is slow moving. Water lilies decorate the edges, and the far side is thick with willows and hawthorn. Swans enjoy the easy movement of the waters and feed on herbs at the shallow-bottomed river's edge, while the calls of waterhens come from the reeds. Ahead a railway viaduct taking the Kilkenny to Waterford line across the Nore comes into view. Look out for the remains of a fish-weir in the river consisting of a tiny green island and a series of rocks just below the surface. Such weirs are a feature of rivers like the Nore, and were first constructed by monks, brought in by the Normans, who established monasteries such as the nearby Jerpoint Abbey.

As you near the railway viaduct, built in 1875, its great height becomes clear; the steel lattice bridge, spanning massive towers of coursed limestone and granite, takes trains across the river 20 m above its surface. Beyond the viaduct are more meadows, flat and fertile, which eons ago formed the bottom of the ancient Nore, the old banks of which can be seen a hundred metres or more 'inland' from the present river's edge.

About 20 minutes after setting out, look out to the left for the castellated tower of Jerpoint Abbey rising from behind the hill ahead. The abbey was founded in the late 12th century and run by the Cistercians, who carved out good farming land from the undeveloped Irish countryside of the time, and constructed watermills and developed fish-weirs on the Nore and its tributaries, the remains of some of which can still be seen.

Soon the Little Arrigle river joins the Nore on the other side, and upstream, beyond the remains of another weir that could have been built by those first Cistercians, the river slows and broadens, and feeding fish lazily leap from the water. A little further on and before reaching the next stand of crack willows, look for an ivy-covered ruin on the far side of the river, about 800 m from Jerpoint Abbey. This is almost all that remains of the medieval Norman town of Newtown Jerpoint, or *Nova · Villa Jeriponte*, founded about A.D. 1200. Aerial photographs show grassy mounds and humps that are traces of the buildings and streets of the town, which fell into ruin after the closing of Jerpoint Abbey in 1542.

Further on the early 18th-century Jerpoint House, surrounded by a fine stand of trees, can be seen overlooking the river. An example of yet another elaborate but ruined fish-weir, like the piers of a bridge rising from the water, can be seen soon after as the river swings around towards the north-west.

There was some very long wet grass in the riverside meadows at this stage when I walked, and although the day was fine and warm, I got rather wet; but as a consolation I wafted along in the heady perfume of the meadowsweet which formed a bank between the vague pathway and the river. Soon part of the Mount Juliet golf course can be seen on the far bank, and the sometimes indistinct path continues through bracken along the edge of a wood. A large and noisy cascading weir appears ahead, signalling the beginning of the Mount Juliet demesne and the end of this walk. I found it a pleasure to sit at the base of an oak tree, surrounded by wildflowers, and watch the grey wagtails seemingly skipping along the glass-like water pouring over the weir.

◆ WALK 28: THE RIVER NORE: FROM THOMASTOWN TO INISTIOGE, CO. KILKENNY ◆

A challenging trek of great contrasts brings you downriver by pastures, meadows and thick woods, passing ancient weirs and castles, to the village of Inistioge, with an optional loop high above the river through the demesne of Woodstock House, owned now by the Forestry Service and open to the public. There is plenty to see and do, so this walk could be completed in a leisurely way by giving it two days, staying overnight in one of the good range of B & Bs Inistioge can provide, before returning to Thomastown the second day.

Walking time: 4½ hours to Inistioge including a loop through Woodstock demesne; allow about 3 hours to return to Thomastown
Terrain: Very variable, from anglers' paths with good stiles to gravel roads and even a

little tarmac; Daingean Wood in summertime provides a short and very challenging section of almost impenetrable Amazonian jungle which requires agility and sure-footedness; I recommend a stout stick to take the place of a machete! There are some fences where stiles have not been provided, and gates must be used; please leave them as you find them.

Suitability: I would suggest that this walk is not suitable for children.

How to get there: Thomastown is on the R700, 18 km south-east of Kilkenny.

Map: OS Half-inch Sheet 19

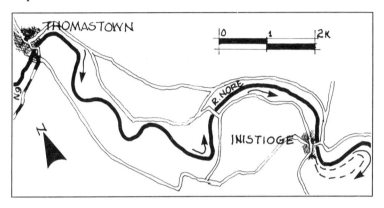

Take the R700 (New Ross) road out of Thomastown. After about 800 m look out for a lay-by on the right with a sign indicating a viewing point; it overlooks a ruined castle on the far bank of the Nore.

About 150 m further on there is a farm lane down to the right; walk down it, respecting the signed request to keep to stiles and gates, go straight over two stiles, turn right and walk down under a stone arch and on to the riverbank. In a pasture on the far side of the river, yellowed by buttercups and rough hawkbit when I passed, stands the untypical form of Grennan Castle, with a thatch of ivy. Built in the 13th century by Thomas Fitz Anthony, the founder of Thomastown, it has a vaulted ground floor and a great hall on the first floor. It was besieged by Cromwellian forces in 1650, surrendering after two days.

Follow the riverbank downstream through a narrow meadow; the far bank of the river, a high escarpment which directs the river around towards the east, is hidden by a thick wood. At the end of a pasture a stile is crossed on to a narrow path through Daingean Wood. The first part of the wood is quite all right, full of bluebells, herb robert and wild garlic in summertime, but it soon deteriorates, with fallen trees and hidden streams to be negotiated as the path seems to disappear under stands of nettles and tall tropical-looking grasses. To the left rises a rocky escarpment, while to the right the bank is separated from the river by a kind of mangrove swamp.

After about 15 or 20 minutes of hard going, however, the path becomes civilised again, and soon you are out of the wood into a pleasant pasture. On the far side of the river now a tall medieval tower rises. This is Dysart Castle, which was once the fortified tower of a church. It is said that the philosopher Bishop George Berkeley was born here in 1685. During his lifetime he travelled extensively in Europe and America, and greatly influenced philosophical thought; the well-known Berkeley College in the United States is named after him. The structures in the river below the castle are probably the remains of an elaborate fish-weir that may originally date back to the 13th century.

This is a most rewarding stretch after the ordeal of the 'Amazon'; a broad wildflower-strewn meadow follows the river as it turns sharply to the left against a rocky cliff and then veers around to the right again. When I walked here, electric-blue damselflies cruised along the water's edge while a queue of swallows swooped and dipped their way along the river's calm surface.

Soon another stile is crossed to enter another tree-lined section of riverbank; this is a short stretch and not as bad as the lately negotiated 'Amazon', but where the cliff-face projects into the river you do have to take a little detour uphill away from the water's edge for 50 m before returning down at the first opportunity. An open space is crossed beneath a colourful house with ornate ogee-arched windows.

The well-treed parkland on the far side of the river now belongs to the demesne of Coolmore, a fine late Georgian house. Up to the left after a short while Brownsbarn House can be seen, a Victorian Gothic house with many finials and weathervanes, to the designs of Sir Thomas Deane. Further on the river seems to descend a series of rapids, before slowing dramatically and veering around sharply to the left again. I saw a salmon fisherman wading in the almost still waters here catch a 4 lb salmon.

Nearly 2 hours after leaving Thomastown, Brownsbarn bridge is reached. Cross the bridge and descend to the far riverbank by way of a flight of steps. As the river bears around to the right through a meadow of flowers and waving grasses, a brief glimpse is had ahead of the far-off flanks of Brandon Hill. On the far side a waterfall cascades from the top of the 12 m-high shrub-clothed cliffs to the river below.

Further on there are the remains of an ancient weir in the river, the first in a series between Brownsbarn bridge and Inistioge, probably originally built at carefully selected sites by medieval Augustinian monks from the priory there. Today you may meet anglers anywhere along the banks of the Nore seeking salmon or trout. Along here I experienced for the first time the wonderful sight of a salmon leaping a weir, a long gleam of blue-fringed silver sailing over the surface of the water in a lazy arch.

Not far from Inistioge look out for a pair of giant alders, the biggest I can remember ever seeing. A third lies near by, having finally succumbed to a high wind.

Soon the course of the river is steered south by Kilcross Hill, and the 18th-century ten-arch bridge at Inistioge, with the forested backdrop of the Woodstock demesne, comes into view ahead. Bit by bit the village reveals itself across a pasture, dominated by three ecclesiastical buildings. The 15th-century ruined Priory of SS Mary and Columba, an Augustinian foundation originally established by Thomas Fitz Anthony, stands beside the 19th-century Church of Ireland church which incorporates a tower of the priory, and to the left is the gable of the 20th-century Catholic church.

A stile brings you to a riverside park where you may wish to take a break. The village has a few old-world pubs and at least one restaurant that will provide refreshments. You may wish to end the walk here, but if you wish to take in the optional loop through the Woodstock demesne (minimum 1½ hours), turn right into the village, and passing the delightful little square, take the next turn left which leads to the back gate of the demesne. Enter and follow the track past a pasture to reach the south bank of the Nore again.

A thickly wooded cliff rises to the right hung down with ferns, ivy and honeysuckle, while a screen of beech trees hangs out over the river to the left. Patches of wild garlic in damp places give the air a pungent odour as they are lit by the dappled sunlight leaking through the foliage above.

About 15 minutes after entering the demesne, look out for a tower-like structure on the right. This is an ice-house with very thick insulated walls, used in the 18th and 19th centuries to store ice collected during the winter for domestic purposes. After the ice-house the river turns south again; keep on straight at the next junction, and go left at the Y-junction a few minutes later. The road now climbs high along the side of the river valley and out into the open, with glimpses of the river punctuated by tree-covered islands far below.

About 30 minutes after entering the demesne another Y-junction is reached; turn right here to begin the loop back to Inistioge via Woodstock House. The forestry road takes you uphill through a young mixed forest; at the first T-junction after a few minutes turn right, at the second turn left, and at the third turn right on to a long straight road through a mature wood of oak, beech and conifers.

At the end of the long straight the ruins of Woodstock House can be seen over to the left. The house, by the architect Francis Bindon, was built about 1740, and featured a central, top-lit atrium, unusual for the time. During the Civil War in the 1920s the place was burnt, along with all its furniture and an extensive library, by Republican forces. Beyond the house and the remains of its parterre gardens, if you have the energy, there are the remains of wonderful gardens with exotic trees, a dovecote, a magnificent Monkey Puzzle Walk and a Silver Fir Walk to explore.

To return to Inistioge, continue on straight past the ruins of the house for another 15–20 minutes to reach the main gates of the demesne with its two gate lodges; just before the lodge on the right, there is a tiny pathway leading down to the back gate again by way of rustic steps and a woodland path.

◆ WALK 29: THE QUOILE RIVER, CO. DOWN ◆

What was once a river of modest size, the Quoile and part of its tidal estuary were transformed into a long meandering freshwater lake when a tidal barrier was erected in 1957. The resulting changes to habitats have been far-reaching; the almost still waters are now surrounded by rushy grasslands, reed-beds and a developing willow, alder and birch scrub which attract their own particular flora and fauna. The area is now a nature reserve, and it is possible to see coots, waterhens, herons, cormorants, greylag geese (in winter), mallards, swans, tufted ducks, wigeon, and, if you are lucky, buzzards and great-crested grebes. Animals frequenting the reserve include the badger, the stoat and the otter. I describe a walk along the southern shore of what is now called the Quoile Pondage, taking in a particularly good little visitors' centre which has great displays that children will find fascinating.

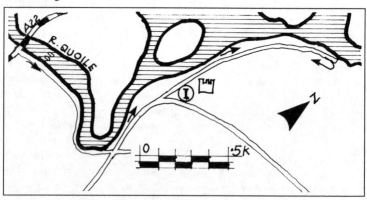

Time: 1 hour and 25 minutes there and back
Terrain: Recently constructed gravel riverside path, a little muddy sometimes.
How to get there: Take the A22 out of Downpatrick towards Killyleagh. After passing a broad area of water on your left, turn right before the Quoile bridge, and after a couple of hundred metres park at a lay-by on the right side of the road.
Map: NIOS Discoverer Series Sheet 21

Cross the road and go through an opening to reach a riverside path near the old floodgates. Follow the path downstream as it drops below the level of the road, passing a series of timber platforms built out over the marsh for the use of anglers.

After a short distance Quoile Quay is reached. Much of the original harbour here, built in 1717 to serve Downpatrick, is now beneath the new road, but part of the quay wall, with its large bollards for tying up ships, remains. Sailing vessels were still unloading coal at this quay in the 1930s.

At the far end of the quay there is a welcome drop down some steep and well-worn limestone steps to a pathway which runs along the shore just above water level. On the right, embedded in the ground like the skeleton of some great dinosaur, lie the remains of a sailing schooner which have mouldered here since 1922. The ribs and great keel, joined by iron spikes, are made from oak, while the thick planking is pine, held to the ribs by wooden dowels. The ground beneath the path and up to the road wall, now well colonised by ash, hawthorn, willow and a myriad of grasses and herbs, has emerged out of the water since the barrage was built in 1957; the old schooner originally lay beached in shallow water.

Soon you will see the ruins of Quoile Castle rising inland. It is located beside the Quoile Visitors' Centre run by the Countryside and Wildlife branch of the Department of the Environment, and both places are well worth a visit. The castle was built in the late 1500s to guard over the river access to Downpatrick. Part of it collapsed in 1977, but some renovations have been carried out and it is now open to the public; the visitors' centre has fascinating displays of the wildlife to be found in the area.

Bullrushes with their characteristic cigar-like tops line the water's edge in places, and the path wends its way between colonising shrubs like snowberry and hazel. Watch out for cormorants, with their wings outstretched to dry, perched on posts on the far side of the waterway; as the channel narrows and broadens, look out for a boulder on the left side of the path with three strange and deeply engraved oval marks on its surface. Are they the footprints of a dinosaur or the devil?

As the scene ahead opens up to display a landscape of rolling green drumlins, the path abruptly comes to an end at the Steamboat Quay, from where a paddleboat service to Liverpool once operated in the 19th century. The riverbanks further downstream are closed to the public to protect the wildlife, but this raised quay is a great place to look out for birds and animals; when I walked here a man told me he had seen a pair of otters near by a short while before. You can retrace your steps from here or climb the steps to the Quay road which will take you back to the start.

THE RIVER SHANNON

The River Shannon (340 km in length) is the longest river in the British Isles. Wide and gently flowing for most of its length, the river and the fifteen lakes which it flows into along its way is navigable for 260 km. It has played an important part in the country's early history, providing a trade conduit from the west into the interior and on to the north, and a back door for marauding Scandinavian pirates. In Napoleonic times an invasion by the same route was feared and led to substantial funds being devoted to the construction of fortifications along its length.

♦ WALK 30: THE RIVER SHANNON: FROM MEELICK TO PORTUMNA, CO. GALWAY ♦

This walk follows the majestic Shannon out into a broad low-lying wilderness far from roads and houses, along a fine embankment constructed as part of the Shannon Scheme. For this walk you will need a group with two cars or to have a lift arranged back from Portumna.

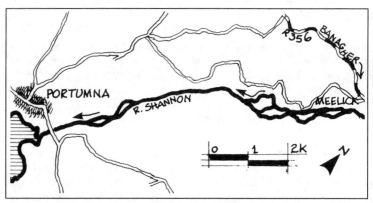

Walking time: 5 hours one way
Terrain: Grassy paths, and a few low fences, some with stiles.
How to get there: Take the R356 west out of the town of Banagher, Co. Offaly. Take the first turn left nearly 2.5 km from Banagher down a narrow winding road. After about 1.5 km the road meets the Shannon near Meelick where there is a riverside car park.
Map: OS Half-inch Sheet 15

Follow a mucky path downstream past a great rushing weir, and climb a stile out on to the Shannon embankment. This place was teeming with birds when I passed, sporting and singing about the thick bushes that margined the river. The river is not as narrow as it looks here; what you can see across it are wooded islands, some of which have elaborate forts and batteries built during the Napoleonic Wars to guard against a French invasion. In a few minutes the path comes out into the open, and the ivy-clad bulk of a Martello tower can be seen rising from the trees on one of the islands, while the gable of Meelick church, with its window of flowing tracery, appears inland to the right.

There has been a church at this place since ancient times when, before the advent of bridges, it was, with Keelogue, one of the few fording points of the lower Shannon. The present building has been in continuous use since it was built in the 15th century.

The path meets and follows a road for a while as the river veers gently to the west, leaving the islands behind, and for the first time you can see the far bank. In places you may come upon small herds of sheep; they will run before you until they reach the next fence. In this case go slowly and quietly so they do not panic; they will stream around you and go back to where they were. The soft, cropped grass of the path, that a companion of mine likened to a billiard table, is the work of these kind sheep!

Along here you will hear the familiar calls of curlews and other calls less familiar; the sky seems vast, because there is no high ground for miles. Millennia ago this entire river basin must have resembled the mangrove swamps of Florida, a broad network of rivers, islands and lakes, creating a major physical division between the higher ground of Galway and Clare and the rest of Ireland. The finding of ancient and sometimes very large dug-out canoes in bogs in Offaly, east Galway and Clare are evidence that much trading occurred back and forth across this inland sea.

Where the Fahy river enters the Shannon from the west, the embankment detours a few hundred metres 'inland', before returning out to the Shannon bank. Note how the surface of the water in the drainage ditch on the 'inland' side of the dyke is considerably lower than the Shannon itself; so when a tributary joins the river, the main embankment has to follow it upstream to maintain the level.

Other than the infrequent cruisers passing by on the river, one of the few signs of human activity along this stretch is a small boat club that you pass by opposite long jungle-like Ballymacegan Island. When you reach it you will be about halfway to Portumna, and it is pleasant to sit on the little timber pier for a rest and some refreshments.

Leaving the boat club behind, the silhouette of the chimneys and castellations of a tall castle can be seen rising above the landscape ahead. This is Derryhiveney Castle, built by the O'Maddens in 1643 and one of the last surviving true castles to be built in Ireland. It is one of the very few buildings to be seen along this last stretch to Portumna, which gives the walk a wonderfully remote character.

After negotiating another tributary inlet, an island almost 1.5 km in length, called appropriately Long Island, is passed. Before the Shannon Scheme construction work there was a ford at the northern end called White's Ford; it is thought that in the winter of 1602 the chieftain O'Sullivan Beare led many hundreds of his clan across the Shannon here, having found the ferries at Portumna well defended. The ford was in flood, so they had to construct curraghs from the skins of hurriedly slaughtered cattle. When about half of the party had crossed, those who remained on the east shore were attacked by the McEgan clan, while those on the west bank were set upon by the O'Maddens of Derryhiveney. After fierce fighting, during which the chief of the McEgan clan was killed, O'Sullivan Beare managed to get most of his people across the river and away towards Aughrim.

After passing Portland Island, a cluster of cabin cruisers a long way ahead can be seen signalling Portumna is at hand. A footbridge is crossed over a tributary, and soon the path takes you up to Munster Harbour, which is just 10 minutes from the centre of the town. If you are still anxious for more, a stroll along the shores of Lough Derg in the grounds of majestic Portumna Castle should satisfy.

♦ WALK 31: THE RIVER SHANNON AT CASTLECONNELL, CO. LIMERICK ♦

The attractive village of Castleconnell started out as a hamlet under the walls of a de Burgo castle which was destroyed in the Williamite Wars in 1691. In the 18th century a medicinal well made the place a popular resort for Limerick folk, and since then it has been famous as an anglers' centre; the place gave its name to a particular type of salmon rod. There are a number of walks along the Shannon that can be started at the village; the one I describe takes you over on to the wilder, western bank in County Clare and downstream past the once famous Doonass Falls to end at a pub called the Angler's Rest.

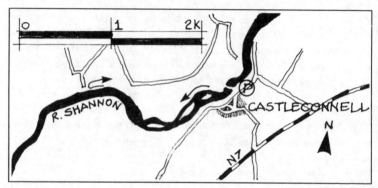

Walking time: 1 hour there and back
Terrain: Anglers' riverside paths, sometimes damp and muddy.
How to get there: Castleconnell is 11 km from Limerick off the N7.
Map: OS Half-inch Sheet 18

The walk starts at the Shannonside car park in the village near the ivied ruins of de Burgo's Castle. Head left and downstream along a gravel pathway bordered by shrubs and flowering cherries. The Shannon is not very broad here; most of its waters have been stolen further upstream at Parteen by the Shannon Scheme (see Walk Number 57). Large stepping stones, probably for anglers, extend well out into the disturbed waters of the river along here; there are many more downstream, some of which may be old fish-weirs, used today for browsing by the many mute swans that Castleconnell enjoys.

After a few minutes a footbridge crossing the river comes into view; cross it into County Clare over a river scattered with tiny rocky islands rich in shrubs and wildflowers, where dippers and grey wagtails prospect for titbits.

Turn left and follow a leafy path that passes between fine beeches and ancient gnarled oak trees, the ground sparkling with stars of wood sorrel when I passed. Soon a stile is reached; pass through it and follow the path across a broad daisy-speckled parkland that sweeps gently uphill away from the river to where Doonass House, a fine late Georgian villa, now sadly unoccupied, stands. The great trunks of a series of gargantuan parkland trees lie, as if in sympathy with the great house, near the path; they were probably planted about 1820 when the house was built. A curtain of hawthorn with an undercroft of primroses and bluebells frequently screens the anglers' path from the house; all the while the sound of the river as it rushes over limestone steps fills the air.

The Doonass Falls today consist of a few hundred metres of tiny overgrown islands breaking the river into a series of cascading torrents as it falls a considerable distance, with a constant roar, making it clear that before the Shannon Scheme diverted most of the river's waters to Ardnacrusha these falls must have really been something spectacular to behold.

Nearly 30 minutes after starting out, a wooded, cliff-like promontory comes into view projecting out into the river; the trees and undergrowth conceal a most elaborate ruined folly built here on a tall outcrop of rock about 1760. A series of concentric walls and turrets surrounds a hexagonal Gothic-windowed tower, with a circular staircase tower adjoining it. It's a kind of enchanted, mysterious place, a jungle of fallen trees, carpeted with pine needles, leaves and the white flowers of wild garlic. It is said that a Hellfire club met here two hundred years ago. Before the trees grew up there must have been a magnificent view of the falls from here.

You can climb up to the folly by way of an opening in the old walls, and find your way down, with a certain amount of scrambling, the other side to rejoin the riverside path. Otherwise you can take a faint path that seems to be a continuation of the anglers' path which takes you up through a gate along the parkland to the right of the wooded folly, rejoining the riverside beyond it.

About 10 minutes beyond the folly you are edged away from the riverbank by barbed wire and thick undergrowth; across a field, however, there is a stone wall with a tiny Gothic doorway in it. Through this doorway you will find a beautiful riverside public house called the Angler's Rest, which was one time a well-known inn. It is a lovely place for a picnic, assisted by refreshments from the pub, before your return to Castleconnell.

♦ Walk 32: The Shimna, or Tollymore, River, Tollymore Forest Park, Co. Down ♦

This is a fine woodland riverside walk along the Shimna (or Tollymore) river as it rushes eastwards at the bottom of a deep valley through Tollymore Forest Park, with surroundings that change frequently as you progress. The forest park is rich in wildlife, with as many as eighteen separate species of animal, from red squirrels and stoats to deer and the rare pine marten. Bird species include the colourful kingfisher, the dipper and blue jays. There is an admission charge to the forest park.

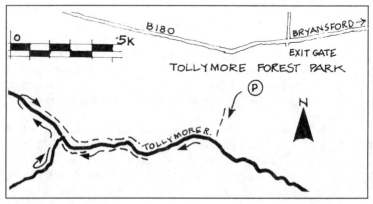

Walking time: 1½ hours
Terrain: Parkway paths and forestry roads.

How to get there: Tollymore Forest Park is on the Bryansford Road (B180) 3 km north-west of Newcastle, Co. Down.
Map: OS Discovery Series Sheet 29

Entering the forest park through its turreted gateway, drive on to the car park, which is located where Tollymore House once stood, overlooking a forested valley with the Mourne Mountains rising beyond.

Leave the car park by the path leading downhill from its south-west corner. Descend between rolling lawns scattered with glorious magnolias and towering trees to pass under a castellated bridge. A babbling brook flowing deep and crystal clear is followed the last few metres to the river. Turn right and follow the path to reach the first of the many crossing points, a rustic bridge which spans the river where it is cascading noisily over the unusual rock formations that make up the riverbed.

The bridge takes you across to the south side which is planted as a modern coniferous forest, quite bleak in comparison to the richness of the species on the north bank. Turn right and follow the path which takes you high above the tumbling waters of the river, which rushes through a deep ravine here. A viewing platform overlooks an 18th-century hermitage built into the far bank. It was the fashion at the time for the gentry to include a number of these strange buildings in their demesnes as curiosities to show off to visitors; in some cases, elderly peasants were paid to live in them to give them a more authentic flavour!

Ascend the path as it rises to meet a forestry road and, joining it, continues south-westwards. The road takes you to Altavaddy (the Height of the Dog) bridge over the Spinkwee (Yellow Cliff) river. Crossing over the river, turn left and follow a side track 400 m uphill to see the Spinkwee cascade. On the way, look out for a homely boulder seat which has a friendly message from the past carved on its face: 'Rest Awhile, To Nassans Bridge 1865'.

A little further on a rustic-railed pathway takes you down deep into the gorge to a little viewing point below the Spinkwee cascade, a white plume of water falling on a tumble of shaly boulders. Towering above the path is an oak tree that seems to grow from the very rock itself; it is difficult to see where the mineral ends and the wood begins.

Retracing your steps to Altavaddy bridge, turn left and follow the forestry road as it passes back into a stand of tall and quiet conifers. After a few minutes follow a pathway that leaves the forestry road and descends to the Tollymore river which is flowing here over greenish pavements of bedrock. Near by the river cascades between a row of stepping stones; cross over here to the far bank and turn right to follow it back to where you started.

This side of the river is a complete contrast to that left behind; here you are passing through the outskirts of one of Ireland's earliest arboretums, where planting was begun by Lord Clanbrassil in 1768. After passing through a fine stand of silver grey-trunked beeches, a rustic-railed path takes you down into a grotto called the Hermitage, seemingly suspended over the river as it cuts its way through a deep chasm. A plaque tells us that Lord Clanbrassil had the little structure built in memory of his friend, the Marquis of Monthermor, who died in 1770. It is a strange and peaceful place to sit awhile, or muse about the many names and dates incised in the soft mudstones of the walls, messages from the past like 'David Milne 1827' and 'Nanny Grey 1886'. I wonder where 'P. R. and W. Munroe' are now, who left a sign of their passing in 1943?

A short distance from the Hermitage you reach the point where you set out. If you are still feeling energetic you can stroll uphill past the car park and through the gardens to the Clanbrassil barn, a beautiful agricultural building of about 1757 that pretends to be a church.

THE SILVER RIVER

The name Silver river is translated from the Gaelic *Abha Airgid*, and the river is said to have been named from the deposits of silver that have been found in it, washed down from the limestones of its higher reaches. So keep your eyes peeled on these walks!

The two short walks described take you on a fascinating journey back in time. Downstream, for a short distance, the riverbank coincides with the route of the *Slighe Dála*, said to be one of the five great provincial highways of Iron Age Ireland, where you will walk in the footsteps of merchants, monks and militias, including the army of Red Hugh O'Donnell which passed this way to its defeat at Kinsale in 1601. Walking upstream you enter an ancient gorge that has changed very little over the millennia, and you walk on old red sandstone pavements formed 400 million years ago.

◆ WALK 33: THE SILVER RIVER DOWNSTREAM FROM CADAMSTOWN, CO. OFFALY ◆

The village of Cadamstown is an absolute gem; there is little to it, but the best has been made of everything by its caring and civic-minded inhabitants. The original village is said to have been wiped out by plague in the 14th century, and subsequently the place was known in the 15th century for its goat-fat candles, in the 18th for its corn mill, and in the

19th for its woollen mill. The Silver river flows through the village, where its banks have been turned into a wonderful and colourful linear park with careful and natural planting.

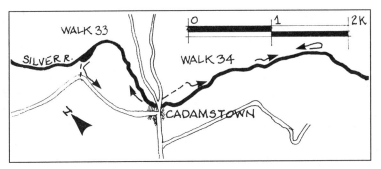

Walking time: 30 minutes there and back
Terrain: Level paths, suitable for all.
How to get there: The village of Cadamstown is on the R421 between Clonaslee and Kinnity, about 14 km east of Birr, Co. Offaly.
Map: OS Discovery Series Sheet 54

Near two picturesque seats that have been made from an old iron bedstead, enter the little riverside park and walk down past the ruined mill building. Passing the house beside the mill, climb a set of rustic steps where a series of stone carvings depicting heads and horses and ancient designs is displayed, and enter the trees high above the river.

The path, bordered by stitchwort and bluebells in summer, wends its way under beech trees, with the sibilant rushing of the river coming from the shaded gorge below. After a few minutes and over a stile an ancient bridge is passed. Although some say it was built on the Mountmellick to Birr coach road, its narrowness and style suggest that this Gothic-arched structure had been in use when Red Hugh O'Donnell's army came this way *en route* to Kinsale, having marched south through Roscommon and Galway, and crossed the Shannon near present-day Shannon Harbour.

At times the river glints silverly through the overhanging foliage and at times it is out of sight, but the sound of its rushing by is always there. The path passes through a small spruce wood before coming out into the open opposite Cadamstown House, a Georgian building of curious proportions.

After a few minutes the walk comes to an end at a place where the river has been dammed to create a small lake; it is a pleasant place to sit awhile and watch the trout, some of them quite large, lazily leaping from the water. You may return the way you came, or follow the sign for the

Offaly Way out on to the public road, and turn left to take you back to the village.

♦ WALK 34: THE SILVER RIVER UPSTREAM FROM CADAMSTOWN, CO. OFFALY ♦

See the map on p. 75.

Walking time: 1 hour there and back
Terrain: Paths and tracks ascending and descending a rocky ravine, not very suitable for young children.
Map: OS Discovery Series Sheet 54

Go to the right of the Riverview Inn which is built upon bedrock, and turn left following a sign for the Nature Trail. At the end of a farm lane, pass through a stile into an open field and follow the track uphill; the river is out of sight in a tree-filled valley to the right.

As you ascend the hill a grand view north-west to the Shannon basin opens up behind; the easiest landmark to identify is the pair of cooling towers at the Ferbane power station 14.5 km away. Look out for a set of timber stiles on the right; cross them and descend into the river valley. Birch, oak and hazel, which must have been continuously present here for thousands of years, allow dappled sunlight through the canopy on to the woodland floor, richly covered with bright green mosses and pale new ferns. On the far side of the cascading river (the silver of which makes you wonder if this is the real reason for the name) great clumps of bluebells had colonised the steep side of the ravine between garlands of ivy when I walked here.

Soon a viewing place is reached overlooking a broad area of pavement with a waterfall where the river bursts its way down along layers of sandstone and cascades over a 1.5 m ledge. If you climb down to the river level here you will find it a good place to take it all in. The layers of succeeding deposits of sandstones and siltstones in the cliff-face are visible for those with an interest in geology, while the liverworts, mosses and lichens will interest aspiring botanists. Although fauna such as otters, squirrels and foxes have been seen here, you will probably glimpse only river birds like the dipper and the grey wagtail.

Further on, a wooden bridge gives further access to river level. Continue on the main track under moss-covered arches of hazel until it comes to an end at a fence, which signifies the end of the walk for all but those with an adventurous pioneering disposition.

THE RIVER SLANEY

The Slaney rises under Leinster's highest mountain, Lugnaquillia, and flows southwards almost parallel to the River Barrow for some distance, to enter the sea after 117 km at Wexford Harbour. There are some short stretches that are walkable, and I describe one combined with the exquisite water gardens of Altamont House, south of the town of Tullow.

♦ WALK 35: THE RIVER SLANEY AT ALTAMONT GARDENS, TULLOW, CO. CARLOW ♦

This short walk is a feast of water, plants, shrubs and trees, overlooked by Altamont House, a rambling country seat originally built in the 16th century but added to in the 17th, 18th and 19th centuries. Children particularly will enjoy the mysterious places, the strange plants and the unusual fowl and fish to be seen on this walk. There is an entrance charge to Altamont Gardens, but you will not be disappointed.

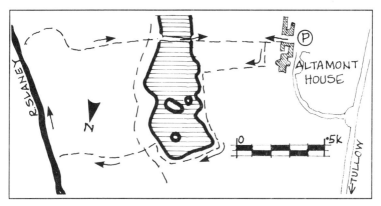

Walking time: 45 minutes
Terrain: Garden paths, a grassy riverside path, and a long winding rustic staircase of one hundred steps; can be a little mucky after wet weather.
How to get there: Altamont House is 8 km south of Tullow, Co. Carlow, off the N80.
Map: OS Half-inch Sheet 19

The walk begins at the Nuns' Walk, a shady avenue that recalls a period when a nunnery existed in the area. Turn left and pass under a yew-like perrotia to reach the formal gardens. The facade of the house, with its sinuous external staircase, overlooks the gardens. This was the front of the house until 1760, when the then 'new' road was built to the west, and what was then the back had to be remodelled as an entrance facade. Colourful koi and shibunkims can be seen in an ornamental pond here, and hens of unusual breeds walk the lawns.

I will not attempt to list or describe individually the range of plants and shrubs that lavishly decorates this gardener's wonderland; you must linger awhile with the little guide they hand out to appreciate fully the pleasures on show.

Head downhill along a box-hedged gravel path and under a couple of wonderful yew arches and past a sundial to reach the lake. The lake was constructed about the time of the Great Famine in the 1840s, giving much-needed employment to many in the area. It is surrounded by a rich mixture of trees and shrubs, an extravaganza of colour no matter what time of the year you see it, the reflections of which double the beauty in the waters of the lake. Embowered seats give you the opportunity to sit awhile and take it all in.

Turn left to carry on around the lake through a wonderfully wild and leafy wood of rhododendrons and variegated laurels. On the far side of the lake, when you draw level with one of the islands, look out for a short flight of steps leading down to your left following a cascading brook. Crossing a track that must have been the old road, a little muddy pathway brings you down into a jungle-like area where tremendous gunneras, which always fascinate children, extend their great metre-diameter leaves overhead. A series of bog gardens and ponds and pools fed by the brook is passed as the path wends its way along through the subdued greenish light that must resemble that of a rain forest.

The path follows the brook down into a primordial gorge of up-thrust bedrock, one great monolith of which looks like a sculpted face. Near by the silver trunk of a holly tree grasps another outcrop of granite like a giant fist. Further down, the path delivers you abruptly out into the open on the western banks of the River Slaney. Turn right and follow the riverbank south past clumps of foxglove and balsam, which you hardly notice after the horticultural experience left behind.

The river, enclosed by trees on both sides, pours with the smoothness of molten glass over a series of weir steps in its course southwards. After a few minutes you reach the return route to the gardens; while in summer heavy growth of bracken and brambles prevents further progress downriver, it should be possible in winter to proceed considerably further.

Turn up into the trees again and climb a rustic staircase of green and mossy granite slabs; there are supposed to be a hundred steps in all, and children will get great satisfaction in counting them. At the top of the steps a seat has kindly been placed to allow you to catch your breath after the climb.

The path takes you through an oak wood and out and uphill across a pasture, through a fenced cordon, which allows you closer and safer proximity to heifers and bullocks than would otherwise be possible. At the highest point of the pasture Lugnaquillia can be seen to the north, while ahead to the left Mount Leinster, identified by its TV mast, is at the centre of a series of rounded hills on the horizon.

At the other side of the pasture a lone and stately wellingtonia stands, slats of timber protecting its bark from the animals. The tree is said to have been planted to celebrate the victory at the Battle of Waterloo in 1816. Crossing the old road again you are suddenly back in the gardens, a picturesque bridge leading you to the Nuns' Walk and the starting point.

THE RIVER SUIR

The River Suir rises near the Devil's Bit mountain in County Tipperary and flows through some of the most fertile areas of land in Ireland, the Golden Vale. The river is 182 km long, and is tidal for the last 48 km of its course, which is probably the reason why it was, at one time, the best spring salmon river in Ireland. At the picturesque Waterford village of Cheekpoint it merges with the already enjoined Barrow and Nore, to sweep in a broad curve out through Waterford Harbour to the sea.

I describe two contrasting walks along the Suir, the first where it joins the Barrow and Nore, and the second, 52 km to the west, as it flows gently through the Golden Vale.

♦ WALK 36: THE RIVER SUIR AND ITS SISTERS AT WATERFORD HARBOUR, CO. WATERFORD ♦

This is a walk of contrasts, between two historic and picturesque villages, that brings you high above the broad enjoined Three Sisters rivers, the Suir, the Nore and the Barrow, as they flow down to the sea at Waterford Harbour.

Walking time: 2½ hours one way
Terrain: Paved roads, grassy boreens, steep hillside paths and a stony shore are all included; be prepared to find some parts a little overgrown and brambly, and a little muddy. The walk should ideally be taken when the tide is going out, although the shore stretch is affected only by very high tides; but most of the route can be covered without dropping down to the shore.
How to get there: Take the R583 eastwards out of Waterford city for about 10 km to reach the village of Passage East.
Map: OS Half-inch Sheet 23

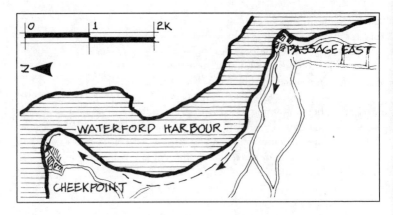

This walk begins in Passage East, a historic village that has seen an extraordinary pageant of history pass by. Near here in 1171, King Henry II, one of the most powerful men in the world at the time, landed with 500 knights and 4,000 men-at-arms to consolidate the Norman Invasion of Ireland. As a young man King John, the Magna Carta king, nearly died here from gorging himself on the delicious local salmon. Richard II sailed up the harbour in 1394 with an army of nearly 35,000 men in a vain attempt to subdue the Irish clans; and it was from here that the defeated James II left Ireland after the débâcle of the Battle of the Boyne. Today Passage East is a quiet, picturesque place, of tall houses and narrow laneways, built right up to the river's edge.

Following the Waterford road as it climbs away westwards from the slated roofs of the village, within minutes the picturesque village of Ballyhack comes into view on the far side of the river, its centrepiece a Knights Hospitallers' castle, and further downstream the river-front terraced houses of Arthurstown can be seen. The river is very broad here, stretching ahead like a long curved lake, punctuated with the crooked and bent poles of a number of ancient fish-weirs protruding from the waters.

The route ahead can be clearly seen almost as far as Cheekpoint; the village is hidden from view opposite the two oil-fired power station chimneys. Before the road bends left and takes you briefly away from this promenade high above the river, the patchwork quilt-patterned Slieve Coillte in the Kennedy Memorial Park in Wexford comes into view beyond the hilly far shore. Keep well in on the verge here as the road swings around in an S-bend, and after a short while on a straight, just before the next bend, turn right into a boreen, the first few metres of which have been upgraded to become the entrance to a new bungalow on the left.

This is the old road between Passage and Cheekpoint, its ancient walls hidden beneath a riot of ferns, woodbine and ivy. Soon a little coniferous wood interlaced with hazel trees is passed, screening for a few minutes the river below. As the gradient steepens look out for the fraughans, or 'hurts' as they are called in this part of the country, the hedgerow fruit that gives the place the name Hurthill. These bilberries or blueberries can provide welcome and juicy refreshment on a warm autumn day.

As you leave the trees behind you are nearing the highest point of the hill, 100 m above sea level, and off to the south-east and south-west there are long views of the Waterford and Wexford coastline. Be vigilant now for a tiny path leading off to the right through the gorse; in a few metres this brings you out on to a spectacular viewing point on a slab of old red sandstone that cantilevers over the river far below. This is one of the few high points in east Waterford and the panoramic view is exceptional. Twenty-nine km away to the south-east, beyond the Wexford coast, the Saltee Islands sit in a silver sea. Due east Forth mountain points its conical peak to the sky, while to the north the bulk of the Blackstairs Mountains and Brandon Hill rises from the hinterland. This is a good place to take a break and enjoy the surroundings; from here you can also check on the state of the tide on the shore further upstream, which you will reach in less than 30 minutes.

Returning to the boreen, follow it as it descends steeply again, and as it takes on a macadam surface, there are some well-tended gardens bordering it to enjoy. The people who live along here have planted the only partially tamed hedges with pretty collections of flowers, and made it a lovely place to walk.

After a short distance, watch out for a branch boreen leading off to the right, and follow it as it narrows down into a bramble-bordered pathway that is sometimes a little overgrown. When the path comes out into the open, turn off it to the right and descend steeply down a gorse-covered hill. Again this may be a little overgrown at times, although locals often tether a goat at intervals to keep down the brambles and gorse! The path passes through a copse of trees that usually has a couple of rope swings suspended from high branches which provide brief but exhilarating entertainment for passing children and adults alike, and eventually reaches river level, delivering you out on to a stony shore near the ruins of an ancient pier.

Turn left and follow the tumbled boulder remains of what was once a substantial sea wall towards a house on the shore in the distance. Willow trees stretch their drooping branches, festooned with draperies of dried seaweed and orange and turquoise fishing nets, well out over the shore, and curlews and oyster catchers forage along the water's edge at low tide.

Passing the house and the old pier that extends out from it, carry on to the next bend in the river where a red light atop a white pole warns shipping of the location of the shore. From here, Slieve Coillte is easy to pick out ahead, while the top of the castellated tower of Dunbrody Abbey is coming into view behind a hill on the far side of the river. Rounding the corner, a less uplifting sight appears, the oil storage tanks and chimneys at Little Island Power Station, and soon afterwards you leave the shore and turn up a boreen into the trees.

After a short distance passing between some well-kept gardens that sported wonderful camellias when I passed, a road is met and followed. Look out on the right for the remains of an old tower with Gothic windows, said to have been built as a folly in the 19th century by a doting father for his spoiled daughter. When the main road is met, turn right and follow it downhill towards the river. Straight ahead is the meeting point of the Suir river, coming from the west, and the combined Barrow and Nore, coming from the north under a railway viaduct that was once the longest railway crossing over water in the British Isles.

Bearing around to the left with the road, turn sharp right, down a little laneway that takes you to Cheekpoint Harbour and its chaotic scatter of colourful fishing boats. To return to Passage East, you can either retrace your steps or follow the main road towards Waterford for 1.5 km until, soon after passing a school on the left and as the road descends again, you take the first turn left. This will bring you back to the 'old road' over Hurt Hill.

♦ WALK 37: THE RIVER SUIR: FROM CARRICK TO KILSHEELAN, CO. TIPPERARY ♦

This walk follows the majestic Suir through rich agricultural land that was colonised early in the Norman occupation of Ireland. In addition to the usual fauna, I have seen otters on this stretch, so be vigilant!

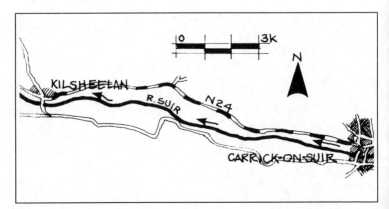

Walking time: 2½ hours to Kilsheelan, say 5 hours for the round trip. There are frequent buses between Clonmel and Carrick-on-Suir which you may be able to avail of for the return to Carrick.
Terrain: Grassy paths along the riverbank, sometimes a little overgrown with patches of nettles, so walking in shorts is not recommended!
How to get there: The walk begins on the western side of Carrick-on-Suir where the Clonmel road comes within 50 yards of the river.
Map: OS Discovery Series Sheet 75

Follow a path along the north bank, a popular place for strolling, heading westwards away from the town. Looking back towards town you can see Carrick's old bridge. A local man, Michael Coady, wrote a poem which hints at Carrick people's pride in this construction:

> Salmon wait for the tide
> To still the weir
> Boys are fishing from a bridge
> Built before Columbus raised a sail.

The bridge dates back to the mid-15th century and was a considerable achievement in its time, being constructed across a broad and strongly flowing river. The fact that it still stands is also remarkable, because until the 1790s it was the lowest bridge on the Suir, which made it strategically very important.

Moored along the slow-flowing river here you may see some of the last remaining traditional fishing cots, shallow, black-painted craft of a type that dates back to the time the bridge was built, and earlier. If you are lucky you will see a fisherman guiding one of these primitive craft along the river, standing in the stern like a Venetian gondolier.

Across the river to the south are the steep-wooded hills that characterise the southern side of the Suir valley. The path is lined with a rich variety of wildflowers in summertime, including purple mint, meadowsweet, cow parsley, vetch and camomile. A long-stamened yellow flower called stinking tutsan is common all along this stretch of the river, growing out of the stone-walled bank, and black and plentiful lacy-winged damselflies dance amongst them along the river's edge.

Soon a round tower with Gothic-arched windows comes into view on the far side of the river. It was erected in the 19th century by the Davin family to guard the salmon weir that was once strung across the river here. In spite of the owner being a nationalist and a founder member of the GAA, the weir was wrecked and the roof blown off the tower in 1921.

Across the river you will see the ruins of Coolnamuck Castle, one of the many tower houses along the Suir. At the time of the Norman Invasion, the Suir was the only safe route into the rich agricultural lands of Tipperary, and subsequently tower houses were built every few miles to guard over the river. Further on another, similar castle can be seen up to the right.

The path along here, remote as it is from Carrick, is often overgrown, and a walking stick can be a useful machete. Soon the rounded shape of *Slieve na mBan* (Slievenamon) comes into sight off to the north. It looks a lot higher than it actually is, 222 m, and is rich in myths and legends involving fairies, Finn Mac Cumhaill, and a high king of Ireland, Ugaine Mór, who is said to be buried under the great cairn on its summit.

Shortly after Slievenamon comes into view a ruined church can be seen ahead, and further on yet another castle, this one sporting a television aerial when I passed, and obviously occupied. This one is called Poulakerry Castle and signals you are close to Kilsheelan. Poulakerry was built by the Butlers in the 15th century, and the little stone-constructed harbour below the castle was probably used to launch boats to demand tolls from passing merchant vessels, which led to the Butlers and other Suirside landowners being called 'robber barons'. When I passed here there were thick bunches of fine-flowered lady's bedstraw growing along the path. It is said that it was used to fill the manger in which the infant Jesus was laid, and it was commonly used to fill mattresses in the old days, hence the phrase, 'in the straw'.

The river now turns through an S-bend; the best route around the corner is to keep to the inland side of the bank, against the hedge, because close to the river can be overgrown and boggy. Around the corner a fine bow-fronted house called Landscape can be seen between the trees on the far side of the river. Soon the grand old arched bridge at Kilsheelan comes into view ahead at the end of a long straight. You can turn up right to reach the award-winning village or walk on to the bridge where there is a grassy area to sit and enjoy the sight of the river sweeping under the dark arches. I have swum here in hot weather and you will often see local children doing so, but the usual precautions should be taken.

The main attractions of the village are the old church, probably dating from the 11th century, with an interesting Romanesque doorway, and the remains of a 12th-century Norman motte overlooking the river. The motte is well maintained in its contemporary use as a shrine to Our Lady of Lourdes.

LAKES AND RESERVOIRS

♦ WALK 38: THE BOHERNABREENA RESERVOIRS, CO. DUBLIN ♦

The Bohernabreena Reservoirs were constructed between 1883 and 1887 by the Rathmines Township Commissioners to provide a good water supply for their expanding suburb. The project involved a significant engineering challenge. The peat-stained waters of the vigorous Dodder river running through the valley of Glenasmole were deemed unsuitable for domestic consumption and had to be diverted from their natural course by canal to pass the reservoirs, which rely on the waters flowing from the hills on each side.

I describe a 45 minute walk for all the family that can be extended if you wish to 2 hours. In the midst of a Victorian waterworks, this is very much a wildlife walk, and to get the full benefit you should be there early in the day. In addition to the usual rooks, grey crows and blue jays nest in the trees below the lower dam and there are also a few pairs of ravens nesting in the area. Along the way, tree creepers and goldcrests can be seen, and the place is a haunt of cuckoos in early summer. Herons are nearly always present at some point along the water's edge, and a variety of waterfowl from coots to Bewick swans can be observed in wintertime. Grey squirrels have recently taken over from the red in this area, and as they are cheekier, they can be seen more easily. Otters frequent the reservoir and the streams draining into it; although I have seen their tracks there, I have so far missed seeing the shy animals themselves. The reservoir is open to the public on weekdays from 9 a.m. to 3.30 p.m., closed on Saturdays but open on Sundays and bank holidays from 2 p.m. to 5 p.m. An entry permit can be easily obtained by ringing the Waterworks Department at 6796111, or by writing to Dublin Corporation Engineering Services Department, Civic Offices, Fishamble Street, Dublin 8.

Walking time: Three-quarters of an hour or 2 hours
Terrain: Paths, roads and one short stretch of sometimes muddy boreen.

How to get there: Take the R114 south from Firhouse in south County Dublin. The Dodder is crossed at Bohernabreena and the road climbs towards Ballinascorney. After the entrance to Ballinascorney Golf Club take the left turn which will bring you down into Glenasmole. About 3 km after turning off, you cross the Dodder again near the back gate to the reservoir. There is limited parking on this narrow road; take care to park as close to the wall as possible.

Map: OS Discovery Series Sheet 50

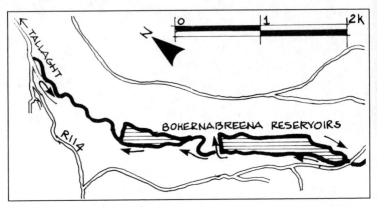

Go through the gate, closing it after you; a gravel road brings you along a raised rampart between the upper reservoir and a flagstone-paved canal, lined with larch and Scots pine planted about 1910, which takes the brown, peat-stained Dodder river past the reservoir. On a mound rising from the slopes on the far side of the reservoir the ruins of St Sentan's church, disused since the 16th century, can be seen. Sentan was a son of a Saxon king who, probably like many others of his class and time, came to the island of saints and scholars to be educated, and stayed on. In recent centuries the place became known as St Anne's church, a mistaken translation of the old name, Killnasantan.

After 20 minutes the upper dam is met; the longer walk continues straight here, but to complete the short circuit cross the dam to the other side. The dam is very substantial, a great rampart designed to hold back the 357 million gallons that originally filled the upper reservoir. Looking south the highest peak of the Dublin Mountains, Kippure, can be easily identified on the horizon to the right with its TV mast, and the deep-treed upper valley of the Dodder cutting into the heather-covered hills.

On the other side of the dam you follow an old boreen, slightly muddy in places, that has recently been widened, with a curtain of hazel, elder and Scots pine between you and the reservoir. Up to your left, as you emerge into the open again, is a series of hummocks deposited here by a melting ice sheet towards the end of the Ice Age. To the right, before the road is reached, are the reed-beds where chiff chaffs and reed warblers can be heard, and where coots and waterhens nest. The road is reached 100 m from the entrance gate where you started out.

Continuing on the longer walk, follow the tarmac trackway downhill beside a complex system of waterways and spillways, and at the first turn right, drop down a few granite steps to a tree-shaded pathway, and turning right again, cross a footbridge over the river. While the Dodder now flows to your right, the waters that serve Dublin are rushing down over many weirs to your left. Looping to the left around the outfall from the reservoir above, follow the path through a little wood of beech, larch and ash. Just before you reach the river again, turn left to pass a shed where floating debris is collected from the reservoir water, and return to cross back over the footbridge. Now keep on straight to meet the tarmac road again.

In a few minutes the reservoir superintendent's house is passed and the lower reservoir is reached; much of this end of it, after successive drought years, has been invaded by reeds and willows, and makes for a marvellous bird habitat. Picnic tables are set along the road in the shade of sycamores, chestnuts and rhododendrons.

The lower dam shelters another little wood on its north side. The road drops down and, emerging from the trees, meanders on like a country boreen. Soon the river can be heard to the right again; we are now walking through the almost unaltered valley of the post-glacial Dodder, whose cliff-like sides of glacial till reach nearly 40 m high on both sides of the valley. About an hour after leaving the public road at Glenasmole, the Bohernabreena gates of the reservoir are reached. You may return to your starting point by the road (keep left all the way, it is nearly 5 km, a little longer than retracing your steps), or by heading back the way you came.

◆ WALK 39: CASTLEWELLAN LAKE WALK, CASTLEWELLAN, CO. DOWN ◆

Castlewellan has been the home of the Annesley family since 1741, and the beautiful 12 acre walled garden behind the baronial-style castle dates from that time. The rest of the demesne, the centrepiece of which is the spring-fed lake, was planted with a rich variety of exotic tree and shrub species in the late 1800s. The estate was purchased by the Forestry Service in 1967, and they have been adding to the arboretum since.

The walk described is around the 1.5 km-long woodland-girded lake, passing a series of amusing and sometimes intriguing sculptures, although I cannot help feeling that some of the more exotic species of trees show better imagination and workmanship! For those with any interest in gardening, trees and shrubs, I strongly recommend a visit to the walled garden which has a wonderfully exotic collection. There is an entry charge to the park, but the whole experience is very good value; a grand little coffee house and an exhibition area are included in the old farm buildings.

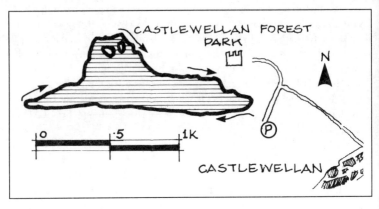

Walking time: 1½ hours
Terrain: Pathways, often a little muddy in wet weather.
How to get there: Castlewellan is 5 km north-west of Newcastle, Co. Down.
Map: NIOS Discoverer Series Sheet 29

Follow the pathway from the car park down to the lake, and begin a clockwise circumnavigation. The lake is broad and deep and surrounded by wooded hills; the eastern end is overlooked by a neo-Gothic castle, home of the Annesley family who have lived here in Castlewellan since 1741. An informal screen of rhododendrons and birch divides the lake waters from the path, and conifers clothe the rising ground to the left.

The lake path is decorated with a collection of fun sculptures, the best of which I thought was the sinuous wooden diplodocus near the western end of the lake. Look out for the pair of monkey puzzle trees before you turn around the western end; feel how sharp and spiky the foliage is, and it will be clear why monkeys would puzzle over how to climb such a tree.

As you round the lake and ascend gently, the Mourne Mountains come into view over the woods to the south. Up to the left now is a stand of Sitka spruce, our usual forestry crop, which look weedy in the company of the more exotic species along the path, including a Chilean myrtus luma with a startlingly orange bark.

As you draw level with a small island just offshore, look uphill to the left; a timber sculpture resembling a Japanese gate stands at the opening to a tunnel through a grove of rhododendrons. The variety of tree species increases as the path approaches to the eastern end of the lake once more, and the path exits on to rolling parkland below the castle. If you do not wish to finish here, I recommend you take a stroll in the walled garden, a 5 minute walk uphill to the east of the castle.

◆ WALK 40: DROMORE WOOD, CO. CLARE ◆

This lakeside walk takes the form of a double-loop through a wonderfully natural woodland with a medieval castle and lots of wildfowl to enjoy. The route follows a nature trail, the booklet for which can be obtained from the Office of Public Works.

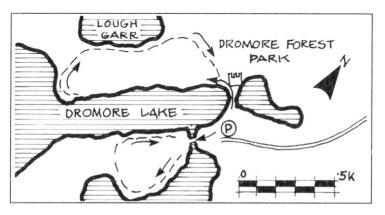

Walking time: 40 minutes for the first loop, and 20 minutes for the second, about 1 hour in all
Terrain: Gravel pathways.
How to get there: Follow the signs for Dromore Wood out of Ruan, a village 6.5 km east of Corofin, and take the first turn to the left. After about 2 km, just before crossing the Fergus river, turn left into the entrance to the forest park. There is a very long 'avenue' through the woodland before you reach a car park with a log cabin tea house and picnic area.
Map: OS Half-inch Sheet 17

To the right of the tea house follow a path that takes you through hazel scrub and out along a reed-lined causeway between Castle Lake and Dromore Lake. From the causeway there are long views up and down the extensive waters, and the calls of waterfowl come from all sides. Swans, mallards, waterhens and coots are common here, but shyer birds like great-crested grebes and wigeon can also be seen.

At the far end of the causeway the ruin of a grand tower house stands, its chimney reaching tall into the sky. It dates from the 1600s and was the principal seat of the O'Briens of Thomond. The stone-carved inscription over the door indicates that Teige, the 3rd Earl of Thomond, and his wife, Slaney O'Brien, built the castle, indicating the strong position women held at the time under the Brehon laws. Every springtime ravens nest on the top of the walls, and when they have vacated the nest, kestrels move in to raise their young.

Passing the castle and entering the trees on the far side of the lake, go left at the junction just beyond the lake shore, on a path that takes you along parallel with the shore, 6 m above the waters.

The path passes through a green world, where all the trees and the rocks on the woodland floor are thickly clothed with luxuriant mosses and lichens. Old stunted trees beside the lake, dead and alive, are like green petrified monsters; it is a good example of a damp woodland being left to develop naturally, as is the policy of the owners of the wood, Coillte, so little clearance of fallen trees or undergrowth takes place.

Where bare limestone is exposed along the lake side, it is easy to see fossil worm tracks on the surface of the rock made by creatures that died many millions of years ago.

In addition to the birds and wildfowl that abound here, there are shyer creatures that you are unlikely to see unless you are very lucky, including the badger and the pine marten. When I walked here I got quite a fright when a much bigger animal than these, a large shaggy feral goat, crashed through the undergrowth and stood observing me from a rock above the path.

The path bears around to the right and reed-margined Lough Garr is passed to the left. Although it appears separate, it and all the lakes at Dromore are connected by a network of streams. Soon the path bears around to the right again, and climbs gently to higher ground where a cluster of great beech trees stands. I am told that these, not being a native species, are to be felled as part of the programme of returning this wood to its original natural state. Soon the path passes through a stand of oak trees which, as they are a natural species, are being allowed to remain. Coming to a fork in the path, go right, passing through the ruins of an ancient house to arrive back at the tower house and the causeway.

For the second loop, go to the left of the tea house and follow a pathway over a little hillock to reach the road. Turn right and cross a footbridge on to Rabbit Island, and take the left fork. This island was planted with Norway spruce, but the ground was unsuitable for the species and much of the plantation was eventually blown down in storms. The Office of Public Works is now allowing native ash to recolonise the island.

Gaps in the trees at the lake's edge give long vistas across the water to other shores. At the southern end of the path, before it turns right and inland, a gap through extensive reed-beds gives access to the shore of Black Lake. These reed-beds provide a safe habitat for many species of waterfowl, from the swan to the waterhen; from the shore here I saw a pair of great-crested grebes, diving birds with an exotic fan-shaped crest, which also nest in the reeds here.

When the shore is reached again the tower house can be seen across Dromore Lake, and soon after, the footbridge brings you back to the mainland and the car park.

♦ WALK 41: GLANINCHIQUIN, CO. KERRY ♦

Glaninchiquin is an ancient glacial valley of lakes in the Caha Mountains at the head of which, in all but dry weather, flows one of Ireland's most spectacular waterfalls, called locally the Cascade. The Cascade is fed by a mountain stream flowing from two high mountain lakes, and in a nearby corrie yet another lake nestles. This walk brings you on a spectacular and rugged mountain circuit of the Cascade and its neighbouring lakes. A local farmer, Donal Corkery, who owns all the land at the head of the valley, has constructed pathways, rustic bridges and a stone staircase of over seventy steps to lead visitors safely around the waterfall, and for his efforts he makes a small charge for those who want to walk here. I think you will find it excellent value for money. It should be noted that although this walk is great at any time of the year, if you want to see the waterfall at its best, you need to be there after rain, when the flow is tremendous. There are rustic picnic tables set out at the car park, and Mrs Corkery also provides home baking, teas and coffee if requested.

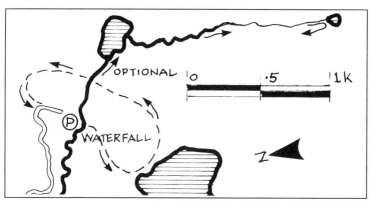

Walking time: Allow 1½ hours for the short version, and 3 hours for the longer version

Terrain: Mountain tracks, paths and open and rough mountainside (particularly on the longer version), often wet and boggy, some short steep sections. This walk is not recommended to those with a poor head for heights. The ascent involved is about 270 m.

How to get there: Turning left after the bridge south of Kenmare, follow the road for

13 km until you reach a signpost for 'Waterfall Amenity Area'. Turn left and follow the narrow road for nearly 8 km to reach a car park.

Map: OS Discovery Series Sheet 85

Setting out from the car park head towards the waterfall and within minutes you will be just below it as it thunders over the bare rock face above in a great white spume. Cross the two streams flowing from the base of the waterfall and set out uphill along a track. Just beyond a gateway on the track, turn right down a rough path that takes you to another stream draining Lough Commeenadillure (the Little Coomb of the Eagle) above.

Follow the cascading stream uphill over boggy ground where insectivorous plants like the butterwort and the tiny red and green glistening sundew grow in abundance. Yellow wagtails skip along the heavily streaked and striated bedrock exposed by the stream; there are a number of pools here sufficiently deep to provide a cooling dip in summertime.

About 20 minutes after setting out, the cliff-girded corrie is reached, and the peaceful and dark waters of Lough Commeenadillure are laid out before you. The name recalls the time when eagles soared over these crags; the great bird survived here until the 1870s, when the last pair were driven from their nests by farmers with flaming torches set on long poles. Rejoin the rough track as it ascends from the lake; note the huge boulder perched delicately on the ridge ahead by the same ice sheet that formed the valley. A strong shout across the lake from here will return a wonderful set of echoes; I counted five separate distinct repeats when I tried it.

The track soon peters out as the Cascade comes into view again. Down along the valley there is a marvellous view of Loughs Inchiquin, Uragh and Cloonee stretching out their silver surfaces along the bottom of the valley towards the Kenmare river. Ahead the strange layered geology of Commeenadillure rises steeply, often patrolled by cronking ravens and swooping aerobatic choughs.

There follows a short steep ascent on a faint path with frequent marker posts up a spur that extends out from Commeenadillure; make a few stops along the way to take in great views and much-needed oxygen. Reaching the top of the spur follow a path along a precarious clifftop overlooking the valley and the Cascade; if visibility is poor it is recommended that you retreat now and try it again another day. Note how the path has been cut out of the thin bed of peat, exposing the roots of trees that died before the peat began to form 3,000 years ago.

After a few minutes you come to a sign saying 'Alternative Route' which takes you to a viewing point a couple of hundred metres away overlooking a high and silent grassy-floored glacial valley. A river can be seen meandering down the valley to empty into yet another lake directly below called Cummeenaloughaun, which in turn feeds the Cascade.

Return to the route from the viewing point and head steeply downhill to reach a footbridge across the river. If you wish to complete the shorter version of this walk cross over and continue along the pathway. If the weather conditions are good and it is reasonably dry, you may want to complete the longer version; allow yourself 1½ hours (there and back) to progress deep into this silent valley, a further 2 km to reach tiny Lough Coomnalack. If so, follow the river upstream as it broadens into a number of pools and runs down through clusters of rock to reach Cummeenaloughaun, girded by a broad band of white water lilies in summertime. Further on you have to negotiate a fence that extends to the water's edge, and continue along the banks through clumps of dwarf willow towards a heathery knoll overlooking the lake.

Follow the river that enters the lake up the valley through thick clumps of grass that can be drenching in wet weather, taking care with your footing. The place has a more and more remote feeling to it as you proceed, ascending gently all the time, with only the echoing calls of ravens and the tinkling of the stream breaking the silence on a calm day.

A number of tributary streams are crossed before, about 20 minutes up the valley, there is a climb to a higher level while the river, now reduced to a brook, cascades down through a series of ravines, which need to be negotiated with care. One substantial and well-named waterfall called Ishgaghbaun (Whitewater) is passed before a higher level is reached, and on this plateau lies Lough Coomnalack, the end of this walk. A short distance to the south now, overlooked by Caha summit at 608 m, the ground drops away again dramatically over 200 m into the valley of the Baurearagh river. Before returning, sit awhile and look back down the way you came, taking in the wonderful and remote quietness of it all.

Go back the way you came to the little bridge over the river just above the Cascade. Crossing over the bridge you get a spectacular view of the top of the waterfall, and after a last glance up the valley, follow the path north along high cliffs with an extensive panorama of the fertile fields and meandering rivers below. A particularly steep section is descended by way of a laboriously constructed winding rustic stairway of about eighty steps; take care if it is wet as the stones can be slippery.

At the bottom of the steps a green road is met making a grand promenade where, no longer having to watch your every step, you can absorb the scenery fully as you walk. Before long the track loops around and brings you back to the car park and starting point.

♦ WALK 42: LEENAUN RESERVOIR, CO. GALWAY ♦

A short but delightful climb following Easdoo, a mountain stream, into a corrie in the northern Maumturk Mountains with exceptional views of Killary, Mweelrea, the Sheeffry Hills and Croagh Patrick.

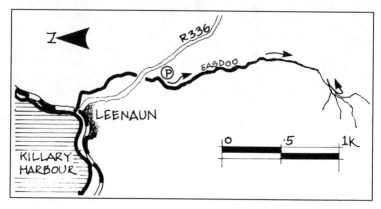

Walking time: 1¾ hours, there and back
Terrain: Two-thirds grassy track, one-third open moorland, very wet at times, and a climb of 250 m.
How to get there: Leenaun is on the N59.
Maps: OS Discovery Series Sheet 37 and Tim Robinson's (Folding Landscapes) Connemara 1-inch map

Take the Maum road (R336) about 500m out of Leenaun; opposite a B & B on the left called Avondale, park in a space in front of a quarry. The Easdoo stream is to your right now; follow a grassy track uphill along it.

Willow trees and fuchsia overhang the heathery riverbank, as the little river splashes and wends its way down a well-worn sandstone bedrock course. The steep hillocks to the right are eroded deposits piled up by a great Ice Age lake against the glacier that filled Killary Harbour during the last glaciation; similar mounds in other parts of Connemara are often taken for man-made tumuli.

The track bears around to the left and a broad, green expanse of rising moorland is presented ahead, backed by the 600 m ridge of Munterowen West. As the terrain becomes steeper, the gorge through which the stream flows gets deeper, and the roaring waters descend by way of a series of cascades. Between the cascades there are deep, shaded pools overhung with luxuriant heathers and ferns, providing overheated summer walkers with the possibility of cool dips.

As you climb, the waters of Killary Harbour come into view below, backed by the Mweelrea massif, and to the north the dark bulk of

Devil's Mother can be seen, with deeply incised ravines draining its top. The track climbs steeply and bears around to the right above a series of cascades that, because of their height, would be celebrated in any other part of the country.

The track now peters out and you must follow the stream as best you can over open, rising ground towards a cirque under Munterowen West. The ground is usually very boggy here but makes for comfortable, spongy walking; the driest ground is usually right beside the stream.

Nearly 45 minutes after setting out you will see that the stream divides ahead into a series of tributaries that flow through shallow ravines cut down through the peat to the bedrock. You can ignore the stream now and head for the rocky ridge ahead. Beyond it you will not find a great concrete dammed artificial lake; when I was here the reservoir was little more than a boggy depression surrounded by steep mountainsides. Turn around and take in the view from this lonely place. A wonderful panorama is laid out to the north and east; the flat-topped Maumtrasna mountains and Devil's Mother loom close by to the east, the Sheeffry Hills raise their summits over Ben Gorm to the north, and beyond them, if the weather is reasonably clear, the monolith of Croagh Patrick can be seen. The only sign of human habitation is a house in a grove of trees up the valley of the Erriff river. This is a place where you need to sit for some time to absorb it all, before returning to the starting point.

◆ WALK 43: COOLIN LOUGH, CO. GALWAY ◆

This is a wonderful circuit of a tiny lake nestling between the arms of craggy Benlevy, an eastern outlier of the mountains of Joyce's country, Co. Galway. It is a secluded, peaceful place, easily missed in its location between the vast and island-studded Loughs Corrib and Mask, but I was not surprised to find that Lord Ardilaun, the 19th-century landowner in the area, constructed an 8 km avenue from his lands at Ashford to the lake, so that he could bring house parties in carriages to its restful shores, well supplied with picnic hampers and fishing rods.

Walking time: 1½ hours
Terrain: Boreens and grassy green roads, with some short stretches across boggy ground.
How to get there: The village of Clonbur is on the R346 west of Cong. Take the minor road west out of Clonbur; after 1.5 km turn left on to a side road. About 1.5 km along this road, to the right, is the narrow winding road up to Coolin Lough; there are few possibilities for parking beyond this point, so it is recommended that you find a parking space before starting uphill.
Map: OS Discovery Series Sheet 38

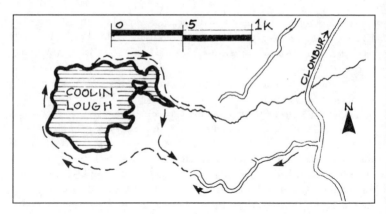

The narrow, and sometimes steep, winding road takes you up into a rough-and-tumble landscape of crooked stone walls, scattered glacial erratics and sparse, wind-sculpted trees. Ruined cottages become common, their haggards and their interiors invaded by fuchsia, mountain ash and holly. As you climb, great views open up behind you. To the south the land rises steeply, with long, narrow fields patterned with cultivation ridges reaching up towards the top of the southern portal of Benlevy, a promontory called curiously Gortnarup (the Field of the Robbers). Soon after a sharp turn to the right in the road, the last roofed house, derelict and for sale when I passed, is left behind, and the road becomes more of a boreen. A little further on the boreen finally levels out and the stone walls are left behind as it leads you on to a broad and open moorland.

As the track loops around to the left towards towering Benlevy, Coolin Lough slips quietly into view over to the right. It presented itself as a broad disc of startlingly blue water without a ripple when I first saw it, but within minutes little squalls shimmered across its surface, as if it had been waiting calmly up here all day to be admired, and couldn't hold the pose any longer. After the tumult of the landscape further downhill, the serenity of the scene here is dramatic. The only sense of scale comes from a cluster of ruined cottages, a long-abandoned hamlet, on the far side of the lake. Off to the north now a glimpse of Lough Mask can be had, with tree-covered White Island and Big Island close to its southern shore.

The track, now a grassy sward on a substantially constructed stone base, passes along the west side of the lake, with Benlevy towering overhead. It was probably built to access the ridge ahead from where great amounts of peat were taken in the 19th century. Soon the first and the most spectacular of the three high waterfalls along here is passed; it seems to plunge off the very skyline, the summit of the hill, before it magically reduces to a babbling brook on the lower slopes. All about, but visible only in certain light conditions, are fields of lazy beds, long disused and eroded cultivation ditches that are, with the field walls and ruined cottages, all that is left behind by the sizeable population that lived here in days gone by.

After passing high above the lake, the track bends around to the left towards the ridge beyond; turn off it on to an overgrown and boggy boreen that leads down into the ruined hamlet of Coolin. Three or four roofless dwellings with tiny windows and thick walls are gathered about a stream that runs into the lake. They are silent now, but if you sit quietly in their midst, imagining their sod roofs and the tendrils of blue peat smoke from their chimneys, you can conjure up the shouts and laughter of barefoot children at play. What an idyllic place today for those of us affluent enough to walk here for recreation, and what a hard place it must have been for those who had to endure a lifetime of hungry winters here!

Leave the hamlet and head for the shore; after a short distance along the stones of the lake side you will notice another section of the bog road skirting the water's edge ahead on a neatly curving base of stone. Follow it as it winds its way comfortably around the lake to reach the little stream at the eastern side. A short distance downstream, cross a bridge over the stream and head across the moor for the highest point of the eastern spur of Benlevy; cross a couple of hummocky hillocks on your way to avoid boggy ground. In a short time you will rejoin the green road you were on earlier; turn left and descend the hill again, with great views of islanded Lough Corrib stretching towards the horizon ahead.

◆ WALK 44: LOUGH DERG, CO. DONEGAL ◆

St Patrick's Purgatory, on an island on Lough Derg in the moorland bleakness of south-east Donegal, became, in the dark ages, Ireland's first 'tourist' attraction. It is said that on the island was a cave where, if a believer was locked up for twenty-four hours, he or she would be purged of all sins for life. In the course of those hours, however, they would experience all the horrors and torments of purgatory. Since the dark ages pilgrims have flocked from all corners of Christendom for this privilege, and today, although the cave has long been lost, pilgrims are still ferried over to the island to endure three days of fasting and penance, albeit in the spartan comfort of a tall basilica. To this day it is not absolutely clear which of Lough Derg's forty-six islands is the one on which that awful cave was found, but it is generally accepted that it was either Station Island, to which the pilgrims are now taken, or the larger Saints' Island.

This walk takes you around the lake shore to join an ancient pilgrims' path leading to what was once a causeway to Saints' Island.

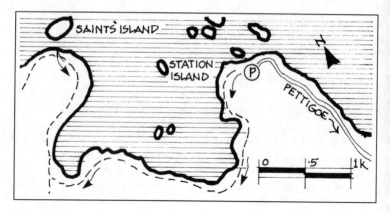

Walking time: 2 hours and 20 minutes

Terrain: Forestry roads mainly, with one short and boggy stretch to reach the shore at Saints' Island.

How to get there: Lough Derg is 7 km north of the village of Pettigoe on the A35 in County Donegal.

Map: OS Discovery Series Sheet 11

You might find it worthwhile to combine your walk along the shore of Lough Derg with a visit to St Patrick's Purgatory. You can choose between a twenty-four hour or a three day visit, both of which involve prayer, contemplation, fasting, and staying awake to do all three. Your fellow pilgrims can be as diverse as fashion-conscious young Italians, rugged and elderly West of Ireland farmers and curious Japanese businessmen.

Set out from the pilgrimage centre car park, following a road going to the left of the pilgrimage centre entrance gateway. The road takes you along the edge of an informal woodland of alder, willow, birch and conifers, where banks of pink rosebay willowherb were colourfully blooming when I passed. Off to the right, as if floating on the lake Venetian-like, is Station Island, to which a blue motor launch makes regular trips to deliver and collect pilgrims. The ground level of the island cannot be more than 50 cm above the surface of the lake; not a tree or a bush can be seen; the entire flat surface of the island is covered with buildings.

The road bears around towards the south, passing picnic tables and a large area of harvested forest. It is always a wonder to me the number of plants and herbs that are banished by the growth of conifers, only to reappear in abundance when the trees are harvested. Birdsfoot trefoil and foxgloves are among those that were having a holiday in this cleared area when I passed.

Soon after setting out, the road passes through parts of a mature spruce plantation, the waters of the lake glinting up through the trees over a forest floor that is a sea of rich mosses. Among the few birds that nest in coniferous plantations such as this are kestrels, and if you walk here in summertime you may hear, as I did, the high-pitched squealing sound of the fledglings calling.

About 20 minutes into the walk the southernmost extremity of the lake is reached, and the road bears around to the right. At the next junction, as with all the junctions on the outward stretch, keep right to follow the lake shore. The forestry road is now a comfortable grassy bracken-bordered track, separated from the lakeside by a cordon of alders.

The remoteness of the place is accentuated by the silence, broken only by the lapping of water on the shore, the wind in the trees and the occasional and plaintive call of a curlew. At 15 minute intervals the ghostly sound of a church bell comes across the water from Station Island. Through breaks in the foliage the wooded shapes of Kelly's Isles, two of the forty-six islands that are scattered over Lough Derg, can be seen.

Out in the open again the road swings around another little bay. The bleak hilly surrounds to the lake stretch into the distance on all sides; apart from the buildings on Station Island, only one other human habitation can be seen, a farm on the hillside to the east. Out on the lake a cluster of bare rocks provides stands for cormorants to perch and hang out their wings to dry.

About 45 minutes after setting out a T-junction is reached, with a forestry road that follows for a while the route that ancient pilgrims took to visit St Patrick's Purgatory, called on the old maps the Saints' Road. Our route turns right on to this road; you will be walking in the footsteps of the thousands who, from the time of St Patrick through the dark ages and the great era of saints and scholars, have been drawn to this place to do penance. If Station Island is ignored, what those pilgrims saw as they looked out over the lake to the right would have been little different to what it is now.

Keep right at the next junction and leave the pilgrims' way again, passing through another stand of trees; the peat bog on this side of the lake is extremely wet and poor for growing trees, generating instead luxuriant clumps of bog grasses speckled with the yellow stars of bog asphodel.

Keep right at the next junction also, to promenade along above the lake shore overlooking Station Island and the quay on the far side. As the road bears gently around to the left and starts to ascend gradually, watch out for a forestry fire-break crossing over; this is the line of the pilgrims' way left earlier, shown incorrectly on the ordnance map as a forestry road.

This is where a little penance is involved and you can be a pilgrim yourself! The ruined causeway to Saints' Island is a couple of hundred metres down the pathless fire-break to the right. It is a terrain of grassy hummocks with deep gaps in between, slow going at any time, and in wet weather it is impossible to stay dry unless you have overtrousers. Take good care as you make your way down to the shore, where you can sit awhile looking out over the 70 m of water to the lonely willow-fringed Saints' Island. A monastery was established on the island in the 5th century, sacked by the Danes in the 9th century, and revived in the 12th century. Little remains today other than a few grassy mounds, but some are convinced that this, and not Station Island, is the place where St Patrick's Purgatory was located back in those dark centuries.

◆ WALK 45: LOUGH FINN, CO. DONEGAL ◆

Legend tells us that when Fergoman, a great champion, was coming off worse in a fight beside the ancient Lough Finn with a giant wild boar, his calls for help were heard by his sister, Finna. She was out of sight on the same side of the lake, but the echo made her believe that he was on the far side, so she swam across to help. As soon as she reached the other side, it became clear that his voice was coming from the side she had just left, and so she returned only to hear the echo again; this nightmare continued until, exhausted, she drowned. What happened to her brother is not recorded, but the lough was named in her memory. I tried to get an echo from the high hills on the south side, but succeeded only in feeling rather foolish! The walk begins with a short trip on a narrow-gauge railway which children will enjoy, and then takes you on foot around the lake and up into the lonely valley behind, before returning on tarmac to Fintown.

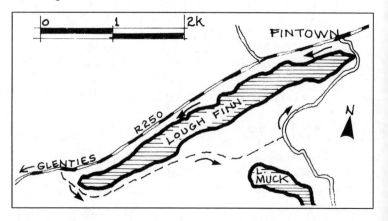

Walking time: About 2 hours, with the help of the train
Terrain: Grassy rail embankment, gravel road, forestry road and tarmac; suitable for all.
How to get there: Fintown is on the R250, 14 km north-west of Glenties.
Map: OS Discovery Series Sheet 11

Turn off the main road at Fintown to reach the little railway station where a disused narrow-gauge rail-line to Glenties is in the process of being restored. When I walked here, the length of usable line was about 1.5 km and regular trips down the restored line and back again could be availed of at a small charge. If you begin your walk at Fintown, you can take the train as far as it goes, and then get out and start the walk proper. As an alternative, but not nearly as much fun, you can walk the road down the north side of the lake. Eventually it is intended that the railway will go all the way to Glenties, but the railway people are very obliging in Fintown and I am sure they will let you out where you wish.

The little train consists of a series of rattling colourful carriages, actually Belgian Charleroix tramcars dating from about 1900, pulled by a diminutive diesel engine, and it takes you slowly along the lake shore. The completed line had not reached the far end of the lake when I walked, and I was let out to continue along the grassy embankment.

The far side of the lake has a rugged, lonely Lough Ness look about it, which makes you take note of frequent squalls of wind that ruffle the water's surface! The embankment passes through a few little farms along the way where you should not forget to leave gates as you found them. The two great hills on the far side of the lake are called Scraigs and Aghla mountain, and between them is a rounded bump called Crockannaragoun which has a megalithic tomb on its summit. With the exception of a dark, blue-green swathe of conifers sweeping down in waves to the lake from Aghla mountain, the hills are bare and bleak looking.

At the far end of the lake a side road is reached and you turn left to follow it around through a couple of gates and past a cottage to reach the southern shore. Beyond a waving reed-bed, the lake stretches its silver surface away into the distance. The track ascends the hill past a little bungalow and a farmyard; up to the right is a primordial landscape of an escarpment deeply carved with foliage-clothed ravines, down which mountain streams thunder and crash. The ruins of cottages beside the track, no more now than jumbled heaps of stones thickly overgrown with banks of nettles, indicate where a small community eked out a living on this lake shore many years ago, probably before the Great Famine.

The track takes on a comfortable grassy surface before it enters a coniferous plantation, a dark mossy place with little else but wood anemone surviving on the forest floor, and foxgloves that reach up over 2 m in height seeking light.

The track exits the wood at the lake side and then ascends towards Crockannaragoun. Rising to the right is an almost vertical bracken-covered mountainside, out of which project great bluffs of sandstone. A little homestead can be seen over to the left in a clump of trees, surrounded by a few small fields that have been wrested from the wilderness.

Soon Lough Finn is lost to view behind as the track climbs between two hills and passes a rocky outcrop that could easily be the work of a contemporary sculptor. Within a few minutes another lake appears ahead, the lonely Lough Muck, lying in a secluded and remote valley. As the track rises again, both Lough Finn and Lough Muck are in view for a few minutes.

Passing by some deep peat cuttings out of which the roots of ancient trees protrude, a tarmac road is reached near a lime kiln, and turning left, you wind down towards Lough Finn again. It is an aromatic road, with the meadowsweet that shares the hedges with clumps of yellow hawkbit and tall blossoms of clover adding to the heady perfume of the countryside. As you descend to cross the Finn river, take in the vista ahead; there are few words to describe the grandeur of the valley running to the north-east viewed from this point.

Ascend to the main road to the village of Fintown; there is a little café here that serves delicious home-made soup and bread and is worth a visit if you are feeling peckish after your walk.

LOUGH GUR

Lough Gur, although only about 1.5 km long, is County Limerick's biggest natural lake. It is an irregular-shaped body of water lying between two steep-sided and craggy hills, and is at the centre of one of the most archaeologically important concentrations of neolithic settlement remains in Europe. Within a short distance of its tranquil waters are numerous remnants of the works of ancient man, from stone circles and house sites to standing stones and burial chambers. Not-so-ancient man is represented, too, by the remains of ring-forts, crannogs and castles. The extensive programme of environmental excavation work begun here by the National Museum in the 1930s was one of the first of its kind in the world. Add to all of this a wildlife sanctuary in a unique and beautiful landscape, and a visitors' centre housed in a replica of a neolithic dwelling, and you have enough ingredients not just for one walk, but many.

It is possible in the right weather conditions to circle the entire lake, but there are some difficulties with rights-of-way, so I describe two walks which may be combined to make one, starting from the Information Centre.

◆ WALK 46: LOUGH GUR, CO. LIMERICK ◆

This is a walk around the east side of the lake to the ruins of a Desmond castle, returning across Knockadoon Hill with its neolithic dwelling sites.

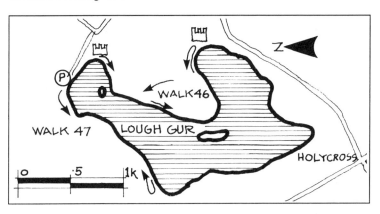

Walking time: 1¼ hours
Terrain: Although this walk begins with a proper gravel-paved path, it is mainly over rough and sometimes muddy paths, returning across a pathless hillside.
How to get there: Lough Gur is well signposted off the R512, about 19 km south-east of Limerick.
Map: OS Half-inch Sheet 18

Leaving the Information Centre overlooking the lake, go clockwise past the car park to reach a path that passes under Lough Gur Castle, which was an important stronghold of the Earls of Desmond. The reed-bed between the path and the lake was alive with waterhens and mallards when I passed, and a heron stalked along out at the water's edge. Just offshore is Bolin Island, an overgrown crannog or lake dwelling, probably of the early Christian period.

The steep and bare, hedgeless Knockfennell which rises steeply on the far side of the lake helps to create a delightfully timeless feeling about the landscape here; with your back to the Information Centre there is only the path you walk on to remind you that it is the 20th century. In the right lighting conditions, it is said that you can make out the ancient Stone Age field patterns on Knockfennell.

After 10 minutes you come to the end of the path at a gate; go through the gate and proceed on the grassy continuation of the path. Up to the left is rugged Knockadoon Hill, with outcrops of limestone bursting through its grassy daisy-speckled slopes. There are no hedges this side of the lake either, only ancient groves of gnarled blackthorn, hawthorn and elder growing out of clusters of moss-covered boulders. The path soon draws level with another, larger island in the lake called Garrett Island, where coots and grebes nest.

The path becomes more faint as it crosses a few moss-carpeted rocky knolls where stunted old trees create shady glades. As it bears around to the left the ruins of an old church come into view on the far side of the lake; it was originally built by Earls of Desmond in the 15th century. The lake side is followed past a tiny reed-covered inlet; when I passed I disturbed numerous rabbits here, sending them scattering and scurrying for cover.

After 30 minutes the path reaches the end of this walk at the ivy-covered ruin of Black Castle, another Desmond stronghold. Although the upper floors are destroyed, the overgrown walls of an extensive bawn and an elaborate gate house give one an idea of the one-time importance of the place. One of its original occupants, Gearóid, 4th Earl of Desmond, who disappeared in 1398, is said to sleep beneath the waters of the lake, and to emerge every seventh year to ride the waves.

Return the way you came, but when you pass the little reed-covered inlet and go through an opening in a stone wall, turn diagonally uphill. Colourful violets grew here in clumps, when I walked here, aided by the grazing of numerous rabbits. Edging your way up 100 metres or so you will come in a few minutes to the top of Knockadoon Hill. From the rocky summit there are wonderful views across the lake. In the distance towards the south-east are the conical peaks of the Galtee Mountains, and to their west the low-lying Ballyhoura mountains. To the south and west the lands stretch flat to the horizon.

Here at the summit are a couple of wide double-circles of boulders; these are the remains of some of the earliest dwellings found in Ireland, and about four thousand years ago would have had low-pitched circular roofs probably covered with thatch from the reed-beds bordering the lake below. A small community of Stone Age people lived in these dwellings and others like them for many generations. Here at Lough Gur they cleared the trees and found the light limestone soil easy to grow crops in, and the lake, which would have been more extensive at the time, a good source of fish and fresh water. I found it strange to stand in this ancient place and have a jumbo jet suddenly appear over the rise and cruise by on its descent into Shannon Airport.

Drop downhill heading in the direction of Knockfennell on the far side of the lake to bring you back to join the path you came on, and return to the Information Centre.

♦ WALK 47: LOUGH GUR, CO. LIMERICK ♦

This is a short, grassy walk around part of the north side of Lough Gur under Knockfennell Hill, with a return past the stone fort on the hill's western summit, through wonderful landscape and with fine views all the way.

See map on p. 103.

Walking time: 50 minutes there and back
Terrain: Grassy paths and cross-country that can be damp and muddy in places; there are a couple of fences to be climbed.

Set out anticlockwise from the Information Centre; up to the right ahead you will find the remains of a group of ancient house sites called locally the 'Spectacles'. A couple of hundred metres on, just before the track goes uphill to meet a gate, turn left and cross a stile over a wall. Circle around a reedy inlet aflame with yellow flags in early summer; the inlet is called Pollavadra (the Cave of the Dog), and although there are many caves in the area (one called the Red Cellars is 400 m east of here), I could not find this one when I passed.

Head out again towards the lake shore, crossing another wall; there are some electric fences here, but they have been protected with plastic covers, or non-electrified sections, where you cross over or through. Knockfennell looms steeply over you now, tempting you to tackle it. Reaching the lake shore, carry on along it, and 20 minutes after setting out, a grassy mound is passed; this unassuming heap of earth is a platform ring-fort. Ring-forts are common throughout Ireland, and were the defended farmsteads of the Iron Age period, although some were occupied into the middle ages. When this one was in use it would have had a palisade or thick thorn hedge around the top, inside which the farm buildings would have stood.

A few metres further on a tiny stone circle with a fairy bush growing in its centre is reached, beyond which is the fenced boundary of Lough Gur House, where this walk finishes. The circle is one of the smallest in the area; the largest stone circle in Ireland, however, measuring nearly 50 m in diameter, can be found near by, close to the Limerick road.

Returning, head uphill for a few minutes to reach the western summit of Knockfennell, where a thick shroud of scrub hides the stones of an Iron Age stone fort; the views from here are magnificent on a clear day. Make your way diagonally downhill to rejoin the lake-side path to return to the Information Centre.

◆ Walk 48: Lough Veagh and the Owenveagh River, Co. Donegal ◆

Glenveagh National Park consists of nearly 10,000 hectares of mountains, moorland, lakes and rivers, including Donegal's two highest peaks, Slieve Snacht and Errigal. The Park Centre is at Glenveagh, situated in a 19th-century castellated lake-side mansion and its demesne of exotic plants, trees and shrubs, a kind of man-made oasis in the midst of some of the most undisturbed moorland landscape in Ireland.

This walk follows the Owenveagh river as it flows down a glacial valley to enter Lough Veagh, and takes you along the shores of the lough to Glenveagh Castle, gardens and Visitors' Centre. I describe the walk from the top of the glen to the Visitors' Centre, which is about 10 km. If you do not want to walk the 20 km there and back, I recommend that you arrange a group with two cars, leaving one at the Visitors' Centre and taking the other the 23 km around by road to the head of the glen to start the walk. There is an entry fee to the park, and I recommend that this is paid at the Visitors' Centre before beginning.

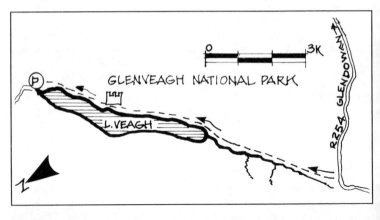

Walking time: Allow 2½ hours one way, but remember there are many additional attractions along the way that will take up time

Terrain: Mountain track, forestry road and tarmac estate road.

How to get there: The Glenveagh Visitors' Centre is on the R251, 12 km east of Gweedore. The starting point recommended is on the R254 about 10 km west of Church Hill where the road reaches its highest point between Casheltown mountain and Meenbog Hill (see Sheet 6), and swings around 90 degrees to continue south-west towards Doochary.

Map: OS Discovery Series Sheet 6

From a tiny one-car parking bay at the roadside near the 90 degree bend, there is a faint track descending gently towards the deepening cut of the glen; follow this to reach a gate in the deer fence and pass through, being sure to close it after you. Deep down to the left the Owenveagh cascades downhill through a steep-sided grassy ravine. It is an exceptionally fine starting point for a walk, and one wonders can it possibly get any better. The insectivorous sundew and butterwort plants are common in the wet parts of the bog here.

Rounding a slight bend, the full and grand extent of the valley of Glenveagh is suddenly laid out before you, with the silver surface of the lake filling the far end, the castle barely visible on a wooded promontory projecting out into the water. The Derryveagh mountains crowd in on the glen from the west, with great skirts of scree brushing the lake shore. The east side of the glen above the lake is greener and heavily treed with the remnants of an ancient oak wood.

Not long after starting out, the first of the series of mighty waterfalls that drains the uplands of Derryveagh can be heard and then seen, falling and spuming down the far side of the valley to swell the Owenveagh. A cordon of oak and birch, trees that have flourished in the moist atmosphere and the shelter of the ravine carved out by the falling water, follow its course downhill.

Gradually the track edges down closer to the river, and 20 minutes after setting out the tree-line is reached, and you pass the first of many wind-sculpted mountain ashes and hollies. While it is important to watch your footing on this sometimes rough track, it is also worthwhile to keep scanning the higher ground on each side of the valley. One of the largest herds of red deer in Ireland roams this park, and small herds can often be seen grazing along the slopes. Because of their camouflage, they can be difficult to spot unless you are vigilant. I also sighted here a pair of peregrine falcons high above a promontory which I found, coincidentally, was named on the map *Binn na nÉan* (the Peak of the Birds).

About 20 minutes after setting out, the gradient of the track begins to level out at the bottom of the valley, and the river flows through wildflower-studded grassy areas ideal for a picnic. Soon after, the track enters the beginnings of the Glenveagh woodland, a mixture of beech, ash and Scots pine, and I was surprised to see one elm tree, a rare enough sight today.

Tremendous work has been carried on over the past few years to rid the valley of the rhododendron ponticum, which, as in the woods of Killarney, had reached infestation levels. The problem with the rhododendron is that it is an introduced plant, and there is no insect or animal in Ireland that feeds off it which would keep it in check. Since it was imported and introduced into demesne gardens in the late 1800s for its colourful flowers, it has spread firstly into woodland clearings, and from there throughout forests, shading the woodland floor, killing off all the plants and ultimately not allowing tree seedlings to establish themselves. In this way it is capable of destroying whole forests. When I passed here, however, the entire hillside was awash with splashes of green, new rhododendron growth, as the hardy shrub re-established itself in spite of the clearances.

The sides of the valley are now very steep, reaching to over 300 m in height, with extensive scree slopes extending out into the valley. A small stone building is reached with two arched entrance doors. It is called the Stalking Cottage on the map and was probably built to provide shelter for beaters awaiting the arrival of a shooting party.

Leaving the cottage, another great waterfall can be seen coming feathering over the top of the cliffs on the far side of the valley, filling the air, as you draw closer, with a thunderous crashing. The skyline ahead now includes a new shape with its mountain slopes, the castellated tower of Glenveagh Castle, projecting above the woodland to the right of the lough.

Beyond another footbridge to the other side of the river, the trees become more frequent and the track takes you briefly high above the waters, before descending to reach the meeting of the river and the lake. The flow of the river, its banks hung down with heather, slows dramatically as it reaches the level of the lake, so they both merge seamlessly. The considerable extent of Lough Veagh is apparent now stretching beautifully into the distance, with the far side of the valley sweeping almost vertically down to its shore.

The track enters an old oak wood, where many of the trees seem to disdain the ground, but instead grow off moss-covered boulders, grasping them with roots like clenched fists and making do with the sustenance gained by inserting a couple of taproots into the soil.

Further waterfalls are passed slicing down the cliffs on the far side of the lake, and the track being followed bridges more streams coming down through the forest. When the last private owner of Glenveagh, Henry McIlhenny, sold Glenveagh to the Irish government, he was not selling a great farm, or even a great and valuable forest; he was selling visual grandeur, for that is what this place exudes.

When the track comes out into the open again there is a good view back up the valley to the top, with the cliffs forming a series of headlands jutting out over sweeping expanses of scree. Approaching the castle now, an avenue of rhododendrons is entered, which takes you up into the gardens. Up till now man's intervention in the natural order of things was confined to the road you have walked, the rhododendrons, and some of the trees planted in the midst of the native oaks; now man's partnership with nature is displayed in an 11 hectare garden where plants and shrubs from places like Tasmania, Chile and Madeira can be seen flourishing.

There is a tea room (open May to September) where you can get refreshments before you continue to the Visitors' Centre almost 3 km further on; indeed if you are tired now, your entrance ticket entitles you to a ride down in one of the regular shuttle buses.

Leave the castle gardens passing through a pair of gate pillars surmounted with stone eagles. The tarmac road is narrow, but a footpath gives you some security against the shuttle buses. An unusual, tightly trimmed rhododendron hedge follows the road as it meanders along and through another set of gates, this time topped with stags' heads.

A junction going right will take you, if the energy remains, a couple of kilometres up and over the hill to Lough Inshagh and on to Lough Gartan. Keeping on straight brings you towards the island-studded, moorland-edged northern end of Lough Veagh, and after passing through a third set of gates and the buildings of the Office of Public Works Research Centre, the Visitors' Centre is reached and the end of the walk. There is a good restaurant here, and a slide show 'interpreting' the area; but then again, having spent the last while immersing yourself in it, you will have no need of slides!

◆ WALK 49: MUCKROSS LAKE, NATIONAL PARK, KILLARNEY, CO. KERRY ◆

Muckross House was built around 1840 for Henry Herbert whose family had been the landlords of great expanses of Killarney since the mid-17th century. The owner at the beginning of the 20th century was an American millionaire who in 1932 presented the house and 11,000 acres of land to the Irish nation. The extensive richly planted demesne, incorporating the famed Lakes of Killarney, is overlooked by tall mountains and has many walks to sample. The walk described takes in part of the Arthur Young Nature Trail and loops out along the peninsula that divides Muckross Lake from Lower Lake before returning to Muckross House. There are many variations and side trips that children can enjoy.

Walking time: 2 hours
Terrain: Tarmac roads and woodland paths.
How to get there: Muckross demesne is on the N71, 2 km south of the town of Killarney.
Map: OS Discovery Series Sheet 78

Cross the road from the car park opposite the gate nearest to Killarney and, ignoring the blandishments of the very insistent jarvey drivers, enter the park. Immediately there is a magnificent view of one of

Killarney's lakes before you, with wooded islands and rugged rocks backed by the sombre bulks of the Macgillicuddy Reeks, with Tomies mountain and the Eagle's Nest in the foreground.

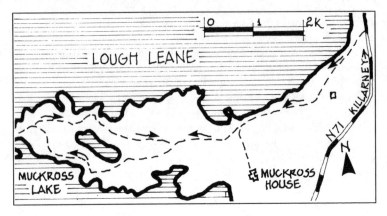

Just inside the gate take a gravel path that goes to the right off the main avenue, and follow it towards the shore; after one or two minutes take another smaller path going through the cordon of alders, bracken and lady's lace to reach the lake edge. If the water is high, return to the gravel path and continue to follow it; if the water is low, you can turn left and follow the stony shore, lined with clumps of great golden marsh marigolds, south-westwards. Looking back along the lake shore the bright facade of the Lake Hotel can be seen.

After a few minutes a brook running into the lake diverts you briefly away from the shore to cross a timber bridge. Back on the shore be careful to watch your footing as you walk; if you want to view the scenery, stop and look! The rocky islands in the lake are ruggedly spectacular, some providing perches for cormorants with their wings hung out to dry. Nearly 20 minutes after setting out and about 200 m before the shore becomes a rocky cliff, follow a path through grass away from the shore, keeping an eye out for marsh forget-me-nots, meadowsweet, speedwell and orchids. As the gravel path is reached again through a thick forest of bracken, the gables of Muckross Friary can be seen in the distance ahead. Built in the middle of the 15th century, it was suppressed twice in the ensuing two hundred years before falling into disuse. Many of the local Gaelic chiefs are buried in the graveyard, as are three of Kerry's great Gaelic poets, Ó Donnchu an Ghleanna, Ó Raithile and Ó Suilleabháin.

Turn right and follow the path; after a few metres, just before a sign for Muckross House, turn off to the right again on to a pleasant woodland pathway, with the waters of the lake glinting through the foliage. The path rises and falls as it wends its way between beeches,

Scots pine, and twisted ancient yew trees that seem to grow straight from the bedrock, giving occasional glimpses of the lake, islands and mountains beyond. The ground along here is clothed in a sea of yellow-flowered hypericum, but in places rhododendrons that were recently cleared are beginning to reassert themselves.

About 30 minutes after setting out, the tarmac road is reached again; follow it until a junction is reached and go right, passing a picturesque boathouse. After a few minutes a great sycamore tree is passed as you keep on straight, past Arthur Vincent House. Where you walk now was originally another lake which over the centuries has been silted up and colonised by willows, birch and eventually mountain ash. At a clearing, the summit of Torc mountain comes into view; keep on straight to pass by a well-trodden pathway near an old Monterey cypress where the returning leg of this walk will rejoin the road.

After a while Doo Lough comes into view to the right; the road here follows a geological boundary line between old red sandstone on the right and limestone on the left. Muckross Lake soon appears on the left. A pathway will take you down to the lakeside at a wonderful little beach, where low limestone cliffs along the shore have been dramatically undercut. Torc mountain across the lake forms an impressive backdrop.

Rejoining the road, after a couple of minutes Colleen Bawn Rock can be seen below to the right, from which the Colleen is said to have thrown herself to her death when jilted by the son of the local lord. The beach here and its surroundings had a very Mediterranean atmosphere when I passed on a sunny July day.

The road climbs above the rocky shore again with bare, heathery Eagle's Nest reaching to the sky ahead. This area is riddled with old mine shafts from which copper was extracted in the 18th century, and over to the right are the ruins of some stone buildings erected in connection with the mineworkings. The roadside verge along here displayed a colourful abundance of orchids when I passed.

Soon the far end of Muckross Lake comes into sight ahead under Eagle's Nest, and after passing Camillan Bay on the right and subsequently some monkey puzzle trees to the left, look out for an arrow directing you to the right on to a track that will bring you back towards the starting point. The Lower Lake comes into view from time to time to the left now through this relatively undisturbed ancient oak wood, sprinkled with holly trees, with sparkling leaves reflecting dappled sunlight. Look out for one great oak tree that has fallen, creating with its upended base a temporary hillock that provides a habitat for a tiny forest of young birches, rhododendrons, oaks, laurel and holly.

After getting a glimpse of the Lake Hotel again between the trunks of tall oaks, look out for a fenced area where seedlings on the woodland floor are allowed to regenerate, protected from the grazing of sika deer.

Soon the wood is left behind and the path passes through a gateway into a rolling meadow speckled with a rich variety of wildflowers.

At the far side of the meadow go through a gate and turn left; the pathway takes you up into a dark and ancient wood of gnarled yew and holly trees, one of only a few such woods surviving in Europe today, where just a sprinkle of dappled sunlight reaches the moss-clothed woodland floor. After a few minutes the tarmac road is rejoined again at the huge Monterey cypress. From here you may retrace your steps to the gates and the main road in about 30 minutes, or complete your visit to Muckross by seeing Muckross House (where there is a restaurant and shop) and Muckross Friary, for which you should add at least another 2 hours to your walk.

◆ WALK 50: THE GEARAGH, CO. CORK ◆

Up to the 1950s, the River Lee south-west of Macroom broadened and spread into many streams as it flowed slowly through a unique everglade-like primordial oak wood swamp, unchanged since the end of the Ice Age. The place was an international mecca for scientists and botanists until, in 1954, most of the trees were felled and the area inundated to form a reservoir for the hydroelectric generating station at Carrigadrochid. Luckily, enough of the ancient habitat remained to have the area declared a nature reserve in 1987, and it still contains among its one hundred species of flowering plants some rare species such as the Mudwort and the Dutch rush. This walk takes you on a circuit around the Gearagh. Much of the area is inundated in wintertime, so the best times to walk it are summer or autumn.

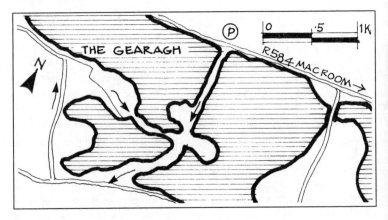

Walking time: 1 hour and 35 minutes

Terrain: Good paths and tracks, and tarmac side roads; wellington boots recommended if the water levels are high.
How to get there: The Gearagh can be accessed 4 km from Macroom on the R584 (Bantry) road.
Map: OS Half-inch Sheet 21

Park at the lay-by and walk out along the causeway across the reservoir. On both sides the scene is very strange; the remains of hundreds of twisted and blackened oak stumps project above the surface of the water, between which, when I passed, small flocks of contrastingly brilliant-white swans sailed. It is like some primordial battleground, where the protagonists have been burnt and frozen into weird shapes.

The causeway was, before the flooding of the area, a minor road leading to a quarry, but now, softened by grass, it serves to access the secrets of the Gearagh. It is a good vantage point for spotting the birds and wildfowl that frequent the area; swans are almost always about but, depending on the time of year, you can also see lapwings, great-crested grebes, and varieties of duck, several thousand of which gather at times in winter.

Crossing over a bridge the path enters a short and narrow grassy avenue overhung with willows and alders and decorated with clumps of burnet roses. Shortly after emerging into the open again you will see a tiny island extending westwards to the right, accessed by a low, stony causeway. Cross over to the island and follow a faint path through long grasses around the perimeter, which is cordoned with birch and willow scrub. The meadow grasses between the scrub, augmented by masses of wildflowers including meadowsweet and birdsfoot trefoil, produced a heady perfume in the warm sun when I walked here, and the air was filled with dancing clouds of meadow brown butterflies.

Near by other smaller islands can be seen, and you may disturb herons as they forage along the shores for small fish. There are larger fish here also; the fertile bottom conditions make the Gearagh a very suitable habitat for pike, and some local specimens measuring 150 cm have been taken.

Return to the causeway and continue on along the grassy path that was lined with the bright yellow flowers of creeping jenny and marsh forget-me-nots when I passed.

About 25 minutes after setting out, the far side of the reservoir is reached as the path enters a little willow wood that is inundated in wintertime. There was once a quarry here which is now flooded, but some ruins of buildings and houses remain. There are grassy paths leading off to the left and right that will bring you, if you choose, to secluded glades and viewing points at the edge of the reservoir where wildfowl may be observed.

Carry on straight at a 'crossroads' and out into the open again with the reservoir stretching off to the right beyond a margin of reedmace and willow scrub. A stile is crossed and the track swings around to the right between two drainage canals fringed with yellow flags. This whole area resounded with birdsong when I passed, and swallows performed swift sweeps along the track ahead of me, hoovering up tiny insects.

Soon after crossing the stile, a fork in the track is reached; continue straight to cross a little stream. Look out on the right across the marsh for great shrub-like and impressive outcrops of royal fern.

A quiet side road is reached soon after; turn right along it. The fields into the right, decorated with wildflowers, look inviting and there are some stile-like entrances, but there are difficulties of bog and impenetrable brambles, so I recommend sticking with the road for the next few kilometres.

Turn right at the next junction, noting over to the left a section of raised bog, which has grown out of the fen to reach a level a few metres higher than the surrounding ground. The road passes Páirc Kilmichil, the GAA club where the first sports event held under GAA rules in Ireland took place in 1884.

At the next T-junction turn right again on to a road lined with fragrant privet, and going by some bungalows a farmyard is passed through as the road becomes grassier, and a stile brings you back into the wilder parts of the Gearagh. A tunnel of hawthorn and willow takes you out across the reservoir again to reach the crossroads passed earlier. Turn left and retrace your steps to the lay-by at the public road.

◆ WALK 51: THE VARTRY RESERVOIR, ROUNDWOOD, CO. WICKLOW ◆

The Vartry river rises at the base of the Sugarloaf Mountain in County Wicklow and enters the sea after a journey of 29 km. The river was dammed and a reservoir created in 1862 near Roundwood village to serve Dublin city, and subsequently a second reservoir was constructed; the two combined today provide 80 million litres of water daily to Dublin, Dun Laoghaire, Bray and Wicklow town.

This is a really pleasant lake-side walk that can be taken in a short or long version along the shores of the southern reservoir, which has paths all the way around it. A causeway/bridge crosses this southern reservoir, allowing walkers the choice of a short loop, a long loop or a whole figure of eight. The land is owned by Dublin Corporation and those who enter (it is particularly popular at weekends) do so at their own risk.

Walking time: Short circuit, 50 minutes; complete circuit, 2¼ hours

Terrain: Paths and gravel roadway; paths in winter may be a little muddy in places. In very wet periods of winter the path at the beginning of the short circuit becomes inundated by a small stream.

How to get there: Roundwood, Co. Wicklow, said to be the highest village in Ireland, is on the R755, about 40 km south of Dublin.

Map: OS Discovery Series Sheet 56

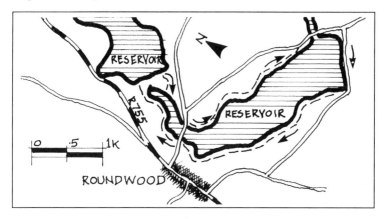

As the road past the entrance to the walk is narrow, it is a good idea to park in the village of Roundwood which is only a few minutes from the start of the walk. Take the first turn to the right on the north side of the village, and after a few minutes you will reach the causeway where the road crosses the south reservoir. At a green gate on the left before the causeway you can start the short circuit or the complete walk. Climb the gate to reach the pathway that encircles the northern end of the reservoir.

Follow the path, which can be a little boggy after wet weather, along an avenue of birch, holly and pine trees. A curtain of foliage separates the path from the reed-fringed waters of the reservoir, and after a couple of minutes, a stream coming from the left has to be crossed by stepping stones.

The path meanders along the water's edge between clumps of gorse, and after about 10 minutes reaches the northern end of the reservoir, a swamp of birch and reeds that provides safe homes for waterhens and reed warblers. Continue on northwards as the path becomes a broad, green track, which leads to what looks like a grassy hillock ahead. Climb the steep hillock and you will find it is a great rampart that dams the northern reservoir.

Turn right and follow the dam eastwards; this is a fine airy promenade high above the surrounding countryside, with extensive views northwards across the waters of the upper reservoir. Grey wagtails (which are far from grey and sport beautiful lemon yellow plumage) skip along the tiny wavelets that lap the stone shore searching for washed-up insects. The heather-covered summit of Djouce is in view to the north, and halfway across the dam the scree-streaked conical peak of the Sugar Loaf comes into view at the far end of the reservoir.

When you reach the iron bridge connecting the castellated pumphouse, descend off the dam into the trees and turn right to follow a track downhill. The track sweeps around to the left and follows a deep and spectacular, unprotected gorge cut from the bedrock to take waters from the upper to the lower reservoir. It is a favourite place for herons, this, and if you are lucky and careful you may get a bird's eye view of one below on the sandy bed of the outlet, preying on small fish.

Follow the gorge back to a Victorian castellated structure built over the outlet tunnel, and crossing over, head out towards the shore of the reservoir again, taking care to keep away from the edge of the gorge.

The path turns south, and soon after the causeway from where the walk started appears ahead across the water, the path takes you out through a gate on to the road on its eastern side. To complete the short circuit, follow the causeway across the water to Roundwood; to continue on to complete the whole circuit, cross the road and another gate on to the shore again.

Here the path follows the water's edge at water level, that is, unless there is a drought; after some recent summers the level in the reservoir was reduced to the course of the original Vartry river meandering through the middle of a mud pan.

Tall slender Scots pine line the margin between the water and the stone-walled reservoir boundary; beyond the wall are grassy fields grazed to billiard-table smoothness by Wicklow sheep. The water's edge meanders informally, most unlike what is expected of a man-made lake, and waterhens and mallards frequent its reeds and rocks.

There are a few damp spots to be negotiated where little streams enter the reservoir. Soon you can see the towers at the south end, and the roof of the church at Roundwood comes into view to the west, backed by the mountainous horizon of Scarr. When the track exits on to the public road, follow it over a bridge which crosses an inlet into the reservoir. I saw a pair of great-crested grebes diving offshore and was told that a few pairs nest here. This diver is quite a spectacular sight in full plumage, with its drooping spaniel-like ears and 'Mohican' crest.

After a few minutes the road takes you briefly away from the reservoir to join the main road for Roundwood; turn right and follow it as it runs straight across the southern dam. See if you can spot a comparative rarity in rural Ireland; there is a public convenience on the left side of the road, opposite the rushing spillover from the reservoir!

There is a good panoramic view from this point; all the Wicklow

Mountain summits from Scarr northwards to Knocknacloghoge, Fancy and Djouce can be seen. Far below the south side of the road the water treatment works are laid out like a water garden in a series of ponds, the centrepiece a stone-edged circle.

At the far side of the dam climb stepping stones over the wall to the right on to a broad track that follows the shore of the reservoir towards Roundwood. I saw a tree creeper here corkscrewing up the trunk of a Scots pine, and I am told there are still a few red squirrels to be seen along the shore early in the day.

The soft grassy comfortable surface of the track and the openness of the shore on this side of the reservoir is in contrast to the eastern side, and even the trees planted here, mainly beeches with a rich selection of lovers' hearts carved into their silver bark, give it a different atmosphere. The good surface makes it possible to stride out and maintain a good pace for the last lap, and soon the three arches of the causeway where the route started emerge into view from behind the trees on the far shore.

Roundwood Golf Club is passed before the grey-slated roofs of the village come into view to the left, and the track crosses another little stream to meet the public road once again. Turning left, the village is just a few minutes away.

CANALS

The Grand Canal

Work began on the Grand Canal to link Ireland's east coast with the Shannon in 1756. It took twenty-three years to reach Sallins, 32 km upstream, and another twenty-five years were to elapse before the first commercial voyage took place, all the way to the Shannon, in 1804. Commercial barges ceased to use the canal in 1960, but its considerable usage as an amenity and the efforts of the Inland Waterways Association kept the waterway alive until the Office of Public Works took it over in 1986, securing its future. The Grand Canal provides a wonderful route across Ireland for the walker, which can be completed in easy stages as follows:

Ringsend to Clondalkin:	3 hours
Clondalkin to Sallins:	5½ hours
Sallins to Robertstown:	2 hours and 50 minutes
Robertstown to Edenderry:	5¼ hours
Edenderry to Daingean:	5 hours
Daingean to Tullamore:	4 hours
Tullamore to Ferbane:	7¼ hours
Ferbane to Shannon Harbour:	2½ hours

I describe below a walk along the grassy and comfortable towpaths of the lesser-known Shannon end of the canal.

♦ Walk 52: The Western Grand Canal and the Brosna, Co. Offaly ♦

This is a rewarding walk past the last few locks of the Grand Canal to where it reaches the Shannon river near the tiny village of Shannon Harbour, with an optional return along the Brosna river, which rises near Mullingar and parallels the canal's course for many kilometres. It was originally intended to use the Brosna for the final part of the canal waterway, but it proved unsuitable, and the canal only joins it within a short distance of the Shannon.

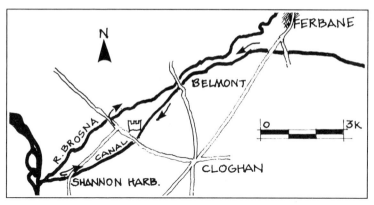

Walking time: 2½ hours to Shannon Harbour: allow 3 to return to Ferbane via the Brosna

Terrain: Comfortable towpaths on the canal, and anglers' paths, sometimes rough, on the Brosna.

How to get there: Ferbane is on the N62 between Birr and Athlone, 117 km from Dublin. The walk starts at the bridge on the south side of the town.

Map: OS Half-inch Sheet 15

Leave the Brosna river behind you and walk south out of the town, passing the gates to Gallen Abbey, once a grand Georgian house and now a convent. Take the first turn right off the main road and follow a narrow winding laneway south-west to reach the Grand Canal at Glyn bridge and the 32nd lock, a deep stone-lined chasm. Looking back eastwards, you will see Noggus bridge which carries the main road from Ferbane to Birr. Leave the bridge behind and head west along the north side of the canal on a fine grassy towpath.

This is a beautiful stretch of canal, more like a meandering river really, with wildflowers speckling the banks. As the canal comes close to the Brosna river again, look out for a great heap of stones on each side of the canal; this is all that is left of a bridge that carried the old Ferbane to Banagher railway. Soon the tall ruins of an old house on the south bank of the Brosna come into view to the right. The road which used to serve it has all but disappeared into the landscape, although the bridge which took it across the canal still stands. The house once belonged to the O'Sheil family, who were hereditary physicians to the MacCoughlans, the local chieftains.

The trees of Belmont can be seen ahead next. Belmont is a recent name for a place that was once called *Lios Dearg* (Red Fort), and it was an important corn-milling centre in the 18th century. Pass by the lock-keeper's cottage, cross to the south side of the bridge and drop down to the towpath; the north bank going west is also passable, but I found it very wet. There are usually some canal boats, large and small, moored at the harbour here below the bridge, and together with the old stone buildings they make a very picturesque scene.

A long, straight and flat stretch takes the canal to L'Estrange bridge, named after the 18th-century proprietor of the mills at Belmont. There was once an inn here on the north side of the bridge, the ruins of which remain. Further on up the road are the remains of the gates of large military barracks built during the Napoleonic Wars. The little corporal was taken very seriously in those days, and it was thought that an invasion might take place up the Shannon; the soldiers barracked here would have been a reserve force for such an eventuality.

About 10 minutes north from the bridge, and worth a visit, is Clononey Castle, a 16th-century tower house with part of its bawn, or outer defences, still surviving. The castle was built in the reign of Henry VIII, and a carved stone beside the castle suggests that two sisters named Bolyn, cousins of Elizabeth I, are buried near by. The place holds a macabre record: it was from the ramparts, in the year 1519, that a shot was fired that killed the first person in Ireland to die by a firearm.

Follow a gravel path now along the south side of the canal. The sad ruins of homesteads and the scattered remnants of field walls all around are evidence of the flight from the land, which seems surprisingly poor considering its proximity to the Shannon basin. The dampness of the ground around makes it a good place to see snipe, that little long-beaked game bird that zig-zags away, when disturbed, squeaking in panic. Soon there is a curtain of young ash trees between the towpath and the canal, while off to the south-east the low-lying Slieve Bloom Mountains line the horizon.

The next bridge is called Clononey bridge, just before which the 34th lock on the Grand Canal is passed. The canal rises from Ringsend in Dublin to the 18th lock, and then descends from the 19th to the 36th and last, just short of the Shannon. Soon the great ivy-clad bulk of the ruined Canal Hotel at Shannon Harbour comes into view ahead, and, a short time after, the fleet of gaily coloured canal craft moored there.

This is the end of the walk; if you wish to view the Shannon continue along the south side of the canal for a further 15 minutes, past the last two locks, to reach the meeting with the great river. In wintertime this will not be necessary as the Shannon swells and floods, covering the fields right up to Shannon Harbour.

On your return, if you are feeling energetic, you may wish to sample the Brosna river. I have walked an anglers' path along this meandering river from Shannon Harbour to Ferbane, but with considerable difficulty because of frequent fences without stiles and in many places along the way dense, impenetrable undergrowth reaching to the water's edge. The stretch between Clononey bridge and Belmont, however, was passable with reasonable ease.

To follow this detour on your return to Ferbane, cross L'Estrange bridge to the north side and follow the road up past Clononey Castle, reaching the bridge over the Brosna in about 15 minutes. On the north side of the river climb over a gate and cross a field to the anglers' path along the river's edge. Stiles take you over most of the fences, wooden bridges over little streams, and the terrain is likely to vary from long grass stitched with nettles to well-cropped meadows and tracks through riverside scrub. Up to the north look out for a hamlet called High Street, identified by a tall square church tower.

A little more than 800 m before reaching Belmont, the river swings around to the left and receives a deep-flowing tributary, an old canal from one of the mills at Belmont. You have to cut inland to go around this; take care to keep to the edge of the field and avoid damaging crops. After about 500 m a bridge will be found across the tributary; cross over and head out for the north bank of the Brosna again.

Across the parkland to the north is Belmont House, a castellated two-storey house dating originally from the 18th century. The cluster of buildings and red-painted sheds you can see to your right ahead is located at the little harbour on the Grand Canal passed earlier.

Continue over a fence to follow a little pathway along the riverbank as the arches of the stone bridge at Belmont come into view. The path takes you around to the left to avoid the thundering mill stream and past the tall walls of the old mill itself to reach the public road. From the bridge you can see the picturesque V-shaped weir, a hunting ground of wagtails, dippers and herons, that diverts some of the waters of the Brosna to the millrace. The great corn mills at Belmont were originally constructed in the 18th century; after being damaged by fire in 1773 their repairs cost £9,000, which was a substantial amount of money at the time.

Cross the bridge and head south for a few minutes to join the Grand Canal and return to Ferbane.

♦ WALK 53: THE GRAND CANAL: MILLTOWN FEEDER TO THE POLLARDSTOWN FEN, CO. KILDARE ♦

The Milltown feeder canal, constructed in the late 18th century, carries the Grand Canal's main water supply from the source at Pollardstown Fen to the summit level of the canal near Robertstown. From here it flows eastwards down through nineteen locks to Dublin Bay and westwards down through eighteen locks to the River Shannon. Although rarely used by boats, the Milltown feeder is kept well drained and maintained.

This is a meandering and peaceful canal-side walk passing the legendary Hill of Allen, and taking you into one of Ireland's most precious flora and fauna habitats, Pollardstown Fen. The fen is a rare piece of landscape in Ireland, where most similar areas have disappeared over the last few thousand years as they developed into the raised bogs that characterise the midlands and west of the country. Pollardstown survived as a fen because the thirty-six springs in the area produce lime-rich alkaline water containing nutrients that prevent colonisation by acidic bog-making plants; it provides a unique and rich habitat for wildfowl and many rare plants.

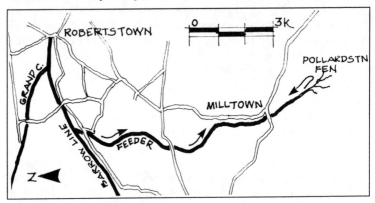

Walking time: 2¼ hours to the Fen, where a pick-up could be arranged at the pub at Milltown bridge, or 4½ hours there and back

Terrain: Tarmac side roads, gravel towpaths and grassy paths; the latter may be a little overgrown, but passable, in summertime.

How to get there: Robertstown is on the Grand Canal about 11 km west of Sallins, Co. Kildare. Take the road on the south side of the canal westwards out of the village; the road briefly loops away from the canal but returns to it before Littleton bridge beside a pub called the Traveller's Rest. Carry on straight to the next bridge, Huband bridge, where the Milltown feeder joins the main canal system. Park near Huband bridge; the roads around here are narrow, so be sure you leave plenty of space to pass, and if parking outside a house, do, out of courtesy, ask permission.

Map: OS Half-inch Sheet 16

Follow the tarmac road along the eastern bank of the feeder canal, which appears a little narrower than the main canal. The waters are deep and crystal clear, displaying in spring and summer a rich and varied growth of water plants.

After a few minutes the profile of a small 16th-century tower house, Ballyteigue Castle, comes into view to the right. Thomas Fitzgerald, known as Silken Thomas, the rebel son of the Earl of Kildare, is said to have taken refuge here in 1535 after his abortive rebellion, shortly before his capture and eventual beheading at Tyburn in London. When the tarmac road bears left, continue to follow a track along the canal. It is a peaceful stretch of reed-lined water here, a quiet home for waterhens and swans.

Soon the partly dismembered Hill of Allen with its tall tower can be seen to the south. The track follows the canal as it bears around to the left towards the hill and passes a wooden footbridge used by farmers to take their stock back and forth. Herons were common on this stretch when I walked here, taking flight at my approach and alighting further on, only to be disturbed again.

The first stone canal bridge met is Pim's bridge, probably named, as so many of the bridges were, after the local landlord through whose lands the canal passed. Cross the bridge and continue along the west bank; the path here may be a little mucky after wet weather, but it reverts to tarmac before long.

A line of old ivy-covered beech trees leads the canal to Pluckerstown bridge where the public road passes; from here the rumbling of machinery in the quarry on the Hill of Allen is usually audible. The hill, formed of hard black basalt, has been gradually reduced over the years as the stone is quarried. It has a famous mythological past as one of the main bases for the Fianna, Ireland's ancient standing army, whose leader was the hero Finn Mac Cumhaill. The castellated tower on the summit was erected in 1859 by Sir Gerald Alymer as a viewing place, and as County Kildare has little high ground, the views on a clear day from here are wonderful. The stone-cutting and craftsmanship used in the construction of the tower are very fine, and the names of each person who worked on it, including a few women, are carved on the spiral staircase inside.

At Pluckerstown bridge cross to the east side of the canal. There are a few gates across the towpath along here to control the movement of stock; be sure to leave them as you find them. Soon the path becomes grassy as the canal follows a raised rampart that gives extensive views to the south. In the early summer there is a great and glorious show of flag sedge or yellow irises along here. Apart from its beauty, the iris traditionally had practical value: the root was once much used as a treatment for toothache, while the seeds were roasted as a coffee substitute. Where the canal bank drops down to the level of the water, look out for otter spraints or footprints; there were plentiful signs when I passed, and you may be lucky enough to see their owners.

Leaving the Hill of Allen behind at last, an old bridge is reached, beyond which stand the ruins of a tall ivy-covered building. This was the main mill from which the village of Milltown, a few hundred metres away to the north-east, takes its name; there were two others in the neighbourhood, one near Pluckerstown bridge and the other at

Pollardstown. This one was quite substantial, and if you look at the west side of the building you will see what remains of the old millrace, along which there is still a trickle of water. One can almost imagine the great creaking wheel turning as the water splashed over it, and the lines of men loading sacks of flour on to carts and maybe a barge moored alongside.

A short distance further on is Milltown bridge, and beside it the Hanged Man's Arch public house and grocery. There is a convivial atmosphere here in this old-world pub, and if you ask, the name of the place will be explained; I can remember only something about a bargeman returning from a long voyage to find his sweetheart had married another, and in sorrow he did away with himself.

Past the bridge, continue along a pleasant pathway on the east side of the canal now towards Pollardstown Fen, which appears ahead as a low-lying expanse of reed-beds. The clean water and good feeding in this canal attracts plenty of fish, and in turn they attract larger fish and other predators such as the heron. Less than 15 minutes after leaving Milltown bridge, where the canal divides at a place called Point of Gibraltar, the towpath and this walk come to an end. All around you now are the tall reeds of the fen, which conceal its riches well; only the plentiful resounding calls of wildfowl and duck from its midst are evidence of the safe habitat provided.

THE NEWRY CANAL

The idea of raising or lowering water craft on a waterway, initially to bypass weirs, originated in China in the 10th century. The technique was first used in the west in the 14th century and it was Leonardo da Vinci who devised the idea of the mitred lock gates that was subsequently used throughout Europe. This simple system made it possible to construct navigation canals that climbed to a high point where they were fed by a feeder source, and from there descend again like the steps of stairs.

The Newry Canal, linking Lough Neagh by way of the River Bann with the Irish Sea, was the first such canal to be constructed in the British Isles, and was completed in 1742, when the first vessel to use it, *The Cope of Lough Neagh*, transported coal down it from the lough to the sea and then on to the port of Dublin. Although the railways and subsequently road transport superseded the canals eventually, the Newry Canal did not close until 1947; the waterway, however, was later purchased by the local authorities for the areas through which it flowed, and a long-term restoration project has been in progress for some years. Ongoing development work ensures that it will soon be possible to walk the navigation from Portadown to Newry, a distance of 30 km. A number of historic villages located along the way can serve as drop-off or pick-up points, and the whole route can then be broken down into the following stages:

Portadown to Scarva:	3 hours
Scarva to Poyntzpass:	1 hour
Poyntzpass to Jerrettspass:	1¾ hours
Jerrettspass to Newry:	1¾ hours

I describe below a sample of this fine walking amenity, where the canal meanders between the villages of Scarva and Poyntzpass.

♦ WALK 54: THE NEWRY CANAL: SCARVA TO POYNTZPASS, CO. ARMAGH ♦

This short introduction to the Newry to Portadown Canal brings you in contact with a rich mixture of natural, social and political history. A new Canal Interpretative Centre at Scarva provides information on the history of the canal and the village, and it is also intended in the future to provide light snacks. On the way you will also pass the Acton Lake Visitors' Centre.

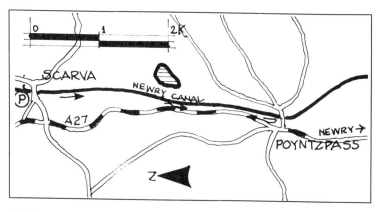

Walking time: 2 hours there and back
Terrain: Excellent gravel towpath.
How to get there: The village of Scarva is 500 m east of the A27, 4 km south of Tandragee.
Maps: NIOS Discoverer Series Sheets 20 and 29

Park at the Canal Interpretative Centre and walk through the village to the canal bridge. Scarva is a neat village nestling under a church spire, with colourful baskets of flowers hanging from every house on the main street. Before the Battle of the Boyne in 1690, the various forces that made up the army of William of Orange came together here and camped in two lines stretching 4.5 km to Poyntzpass in one direction and 5 km to Loughbrickland in the other. Prince William himself is said to have sheltered under an ancient chestnut tree that still exists in the Scarva House demesne; an account of the early 19th century, however, suggests it was an oak tree. At Scarva, an annual re-enactment of the Battle of the Boyne is held on 12 July. Cross the bridge over the canal and head south along the towpath.

Looking back towards the village after a few minutes, the red-painted, Gothic-doored Scarva Orange Hall can be seen. The track narrows to a pleasant gravel path through grand open country; there is little water in the canal in places, but what water there is provides a rich habitat for plants and fauna. There was certainly enough to interest herons when I passed, because I disturbed two on this short stretch, and I was entertained along the way by long-tailed tits, coal tits and tree creepers.

Beyond a row of oak trees on the far side, hidden by further trees, is Scarva House, originally built in 1719. Just past the oak trees, a long grassy bank running parallel to the canal comes into view; this is part of the Black Pig's Dyke, an Iron Age defensive earthwork, once 5 m high. Sections of similar earthworks still surviving roughly correspond to the borders of the ancient province of Ulster, and bear out the story that one great ditch was built in the 4th century A.D. to separate Ulster from the rest of Ireland. The name Black Pig is said to refer to the legend that the ditch was created in one night by a mythical and magical pig.

The canal bends around to the right and passes through a section where it is thickly overhung with shrubs and trees. The borders of the path were wonderfully decorated by perfumed burnet roses when I passed. Swinging left again, the path comes close to the railway line that has been near by since leaving Scarva; look out for the fine wrought-iron gate with a 'sunburst' design giving access to the track.

Half an hour after leaving Scarva, Acton Lake, also known by the more exciting name of Lough Shark, is reached. This lake was expanded at the time of the building of the canal and became one of the feeders for the canal. Not far away to the west now is Druminargal House. Admiral Charles Lucas was born here. During the Crimean War, as a midshipman in the Royal Navy, he risked his life to pick up a live Russian shell from the deck of his ship and throw it overboard. Queen Victoria was so taken by the story of the boy's courage that she created her own medal of bravery, the Victoria Cross, and Lucas was the first recipient.

Further on is the Acton Lake Visitors' Centre, a reconstructed sluice-keeper's cottage. Soon the canal comes into the open again; over to the right, ahead on a hill, is the beautifully sited Acton House, a fine bow-fronted Georgian house. The church tower of Poyntzpass comes into view ahead now. The well-drained and husbanded countryside you see around you does little to suggest that this area was once thickly covered with bogs and woods. A passable route through it, connecting Counties Armagh and Down, was defended by the men of the Earl of Tyrone and breached in the 17th century by an English force under an officer named Poyntz, who gave it his name.

The canal enters the village of Poyntzpass and the end of this section of the Newry Canal near the Orange Hall, built in 1870. The next village on the canal, Jerrettspass, is 7 km further on, and the town of Newry is 14 km away.

THE ROYAL CANAL

It is difficult to understand, with the problems involved in the route chosen and the fact that the canal was for much of its length within 20 km of the earlier Grand Canal, how the Royal Canal ever came into being; it is probably, like some contemporary extravaganzas I can think of, a child of political intrigue and public funding. Construction work commenced on the canal in 1790; Mullingar was reached in 1806 and the link with the Shannon completed in 1817. In spite of the competition of the Grand Canal, however, for a canal system of its time, the Royal enjoyed significant if brief success: 80,000 tons of cargo were being carried annually by the 1830s, in addition to 40,000 passengers. By then, however, the concept of transport by rail had become a reality in the building of the Dublin to Kingstown railway, and the end was in sight.

After many years in disuse, the Royal has recently been restored by the Office of Public Works, and by the time you read this, its towpaths should be walkable from Dublin to the Shannon near Longford town. The logistics for walkers, however, are not as handy as they are with the Grand Canal because, at time of writing, many of the villages along the canal cannot provide overnight accommodation. If it was intended to walk the whole route, it might be best to start at Blanchardstown and walk it in the following stages. (Times are given as a guide only; parts of the Shannon end of the canal can be rough and overgrown in summertime and times will depend on the current condition and number of fences that have sprung up!)

Blanchardstown to Maynooth:	4½ hours
Maynooth to Enfield:	5¼ hours
Enfield to Thomastown Bridge:	6¾ hours
Thomastown Bridge to Mullingar:	4½ hours
Mullingar to Ballynacargy:	5 hours

Ballynacargy to Abbeyshrule:	3 hours
Abbeyshrule to Ballybrannigan Harbour:	4½ hours
Ballybrannigan Harbour to Killashee:	4¾ hours
Killashee to Richmond Harbour:	1½ hours

Below, I describe walks on two stretches of the Royal Canal, one ending in the town of Maynooth, which owes its existence to the canal, and one originating in the town of Mullingar, already a prosperous place when the canal was built.

♦ Walk 55: The Royal Canal: Blanchardstown to Maynooth, Co. Kildare ♦

This is a 16 km walk which follows the 144 km Royal Canal from the outer suburbs of Dublin to the university town of Maynooth. The canal follows a level that is sometimes below that of the surrounding countryside, and sometimes spectacularly high above it, as at the Ryevale Aqueduct.

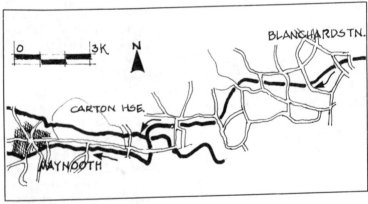

Walking time: 4½ hours one way
Terrain: Grassy towpath, sometimes a little muddy.
How to get there: Take the N3 north-west out of Dublin, and after the M50 roundabout, take the first turn left and follow signs for Castleknock station.
Map: OS Discovery Series Sheet 50

The walk starts on the south bank of the canal at Granard bridge, close to the Castleknock railway station, and in minutes you are following a grassy track through a linear park, with birdsong on all sides, and only the odd glimpse of the roofs of houses over the trees to the north to suggest that you are not deep in the countryside.

The canal drops away from the towpath until the surface of the water is nearly 9 m below the path, and in wet weather care needs to be taken not to slip over the edge. The birdlife in this linear wilderness was rich and plentiful when I walked here; wrens, robins and blackbirds were constant companions, while wood pigeons clattered out of the trees ahead and grey-backed crows and magpies were never far away. In the water below, mallards and waterhens were common.

This deep 3 km cutting, called the Deep Sinking, was carved and dynamited out of the bedrock of a low hill; the bare rock of the side and bottom of the cutting can be clearly seen in places, particularly at the next bridge, Kirkpatrick bridge. The expense of cutting through the solid rock of a hill, which could have been avoided by routing the canal further north, was taken to ensure a connection with Maynooth, the landlord of which was the Duke of Leinster, a prominent member of the Royal Canal Company. The cutting was too narrow for two barges to pass at the same time, and the bargemen used to sound a trumpet when they arrived at either end; if they heard no reply, they proceeded. Somewhere along here one of the worst single accidents to occur on the canal happened in 1845, when a passenger boat struck a rock at the edge and capsized, drowning sixteen of its passengers.

Shortly after passing under Kirkpatrick bridge the canal comes out into more open ground, and the sight of rural red corrugated cottage roofs on the far side suggests that, even if briefly, suburbia has been left behind. At Kennan bridge the route crosses to the northern bank and continues on a narrow path lined on both sides by trees. Clonsilla railway station is at Callaghan bridge, after which the canal runs through suburbia again, and swinging around to the left, passes a substantial embankment and piers of what was once a railway bridge. At Pakenham bridge the outskirts of the town of Lucan can be seen to the left, and to the north stretch the flat rich farmlands of Kildare.

After Collins's bridge there is a very open stretch of country leading to a Royal Canal Amenity Group Centre and slipway which in season is a hive of activity, with small craft coming and going and the barbecue in full use. Cope bridge is a double-bridge, the original construction having been extended with an additional arch when the railway came along. Further on, a cascading stream which is culverted under the canal signals that the great Ryewater Aqueduct, which takes the canal high over the valley of the Rye river, is being approached. This was the second expensive and time-consuming measure that had to be taken to get the canal to Maynooth. The works here took six years to complete at a cost of £27,000, a small fortune at the time. As the surrounding countryside falls away into the deep river valley, there are great views all round from the towpath, with the Wicklow Mountains appearing on the southern horizon and the Rye river meandering northwards.

Beyond the aqueduct are the outskirts of Leixlip, a sea of semi-detached houses, crowding shoulder to shoulder against the canal's southern banks.

The next bridge is Louisa bridge, built in 1794, and about 20 minutes beyond it the impressive expanse of the Intel computer factory is passed to the north. Just after Deey bridge is the 13th lock which had the reputation of being haunted. The old canal bargemen would never moor there for the night. The lock-keeper here is also the level crossing keeper for the railway. A loud bell rings when a train is a few miles down the track, a signal to close the manually operated crossing. However, drivers of stopped cars who become impatient may ring another bell, and if there is time the keeper may come out again and let them through!

Soon the towpath meets and parallels the main Galway road, and for a while the three great transport routes — road, rail and canal — keep each other company. Soon big stands of trees on the far side of the road indicate that the route has reached the 1,000 acre demesne of Carton House.

Carton House is one of the finest of the great houses surviving from the Georgian period in Ireland. Although built in the early 17th century, it was completely remodelled in 1739 after coming into the ownership of Robert, 19th Earl of Kildare. He was described as 'effeminate, puny, extremely formal and delicate, insomuch that when he was married to Lady Mary O'Brien, one of the most shining beauties of the world, he would not take his wedding gloves off when he went to bed'. The reconstruction of the house was carried out to the designs of Richard Castle, and the decorative internal plasterwork was by the Italian Francini brothers, the leading experts in baroque decoration.

As the next bridge, Pike bridge, is approached, an old folly tower is visible in the Carton demesne, while to the south an obelisk-topped folly erected in 1740 and marking the northern boundary of another great demesne, that of Castletown, can be seen. There is a little landscaped canal-side park at Pike bridge, with seats that make it ideal for a refreshment break or a picnic.

A long straight grassy stretch now takes the route towards Maynooth, heralded by the view of the neo-Gothic spire of the College chapel, designed by the architect J. J. McCarthy and completed in 1882, the year of his death. When you get to the old harbour, the centre of the town is a short distance to the right.

♦ WALK 56: THE ROYAL CANAL: MULLINGAR TO NEAD'S BRIDGE, CO. WESTMEATH ♦

The countryside that this section of the canal passes through consists of, in the main, poor land that in the past did not attract much interest or development; non-traditional local names like Marlinstown, Plodstown and the Downs are indicative of this. This walk, however, is an amateur botanist's delight; it consists of three distinct sections, a sheltered cutting, an open bogland, and a pastoral section lined with great beech trees, all with rich and abundant displays of typical grasses and wildflowers. If you do not want to walk back to Mullingar and have no pick-up arranged, the staff at Mary Lynch's pub at Nead's bridge can arrange a taxi to bring you back to town, while you relax and take refreshments.

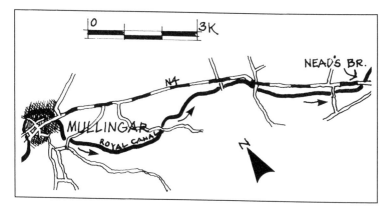

Walking time: 2½ hours
Terrain: Comfortable towpaths, mainly comfortable grassy surface.
How to get there: Mullingar is on the N4, 81 km from Dublin.
Maps: OS Half-inch Sheets 12 and 13

At the eastern end of the town of Mullingar, where the Dublin road passes over the Royal Canal, this walk starts. Head south and away from the hustle and bustle of the town along a tarmac towpath beside the placid and partly overgrown canal. There is little movement in the waters because the canal is at its summit level here, fed by Lough Owel; west of Mullingar the canal 'steps' down twenty locks to reach the Shannon, and going east there are twenty-five 'steps' down to the Liffey in Dublin. After a few minutes at a place called Piper's Boreen, a small harbour is reached where the canal widens to allow barges to turn or moor.

After the harbour the towpath has reduced to a comfortable gravel path along a pleasant grassy bank sporting, when I passed, a colourful display of fragrant water mint and meadowsweet. Saunder's bridge comes into view ahead now, a bridge of subtle planes and curves of neatly cut stone. At the bridge the canal swings around to the left to run parallel to the railway line, which was built in 1848 and within a few years had made the canal obsolete.

For over 3 km now the canal runs through a man-made rocky ravine; the rock excavation needed to maintain the summit level here almost put the canal company out of business during construction work in 1806, but today it provides a unique and beautiful protected linear parkland. Clumps of great willowherb give colour to banks of gorse on the far side, while the towpath passes along a grassy meadow of the type that has now almost died out, rich in herbs, grasses and wildflowers like lesser knapweed, devil's bit scabious and lady's bedstraw. Waterhens cruise amid reedmace and the spiked leaves of arrowhead beside the far bank, and tiny wrens dart from bush to bush. A gentle sloping bank along here is a good place to take your ease and enjoy the peace of the place.

The canal weaves its way through this sheltered rock garden until, about 45 minutes after setting out, it bends around to the left and Baltrasna bridge comes into view ahead, where the canal emerges from the cutting into the open.

In the distance the traffic on the Dublin road can be heard now as the canal crosses flat marshland, scattered with birch and willow. Soon the ground level drops away, and a tall embankment carries the canal; one wonders at the skills of those canal engineers of two hundred years ago, who had to calculate the optimum economic route for the canal across country without the aid of elaborate surveying equipment or computers.

You will note that the flora and fauna have changed since leaving the cutting; heather covers the marshland around; silverweed, yarrow, water mint and delicate eyebright, which is said to be an excellent herb for the treatment of eye problems, are now the main flowers along the towpath, and the curlew with its plaintive call has taken the place of the waterhen.

Soon the canal meets the road and a footbridge to the far side, festooned in traveller's joy, is passed. After the footbridge the canal parallels the road for nearly 1 km, before Down's bridge is met. As you pass under the bridge, look out for smooth horizontal grooves in the stone corner at the far side; these were worn over nearly a century and a half by tow ropes as horses pulling barges bore right with the towpath.

After the bridge the towpath is a welcome grassy track again, and passes into the third distinct habitat type of this walk. The quality of the land has improved considerably, and the first prosperous-looking farmhouses of the day are seen. A long succession of great beech trees, with an under-storey of hawthorn, elder and burnet roses, lines the canal, which was patrolled when I passed by large droning dragonflies.

After a while the beeches run out, the last one being an uncommon weeping variety, and a hedgerow takes over. A counter-balanced lifting bridge framing the spire of Heathstown church in the far distance is passed before the pale gables of the pub at Nead's bridge, the end of this walk, come into view ahead. The canal curves its way around towards the bridge on a very high embankment, under which a small river flows, until it meets the railway line again just before it passes under the main Dublin road. The handsome and, if you are thirsty, very welcome sight of Mary Lynch's family Grocer and Wine Merchants emporium draws you off the towpath and across the road to finish this walk.

♦ Walk 57: The Shannon Scheme Canal, O'Briensbridge, Co. Limerick ♦

After flowing through the very flat terrain of the midlands, in the last 40 km the Shannon descends dramatically to the sea at a rate of 180 tonnes per second. This volume of flow was identified as being ideal for the generation of electricity, and in 1926 the young government of the Irish Free State embarked on the most ambitious building project Ireland had ever seen: the construction of river embankments, a major diversion of the river, and what was at the time a massive power station to provide electricity for the newly emerging nation. The Shannon was diverted at Parteen, north of O'Briensbridge, and carried by way of a headrace canal to a power station 10 km downstream at Ardnacrusha.

This walk takes you along a quiet stretch of the headwater canal, on a high and broad embankment between O'Briensbridge and the village of Clonlara, 4 km above Ardnacrusha.

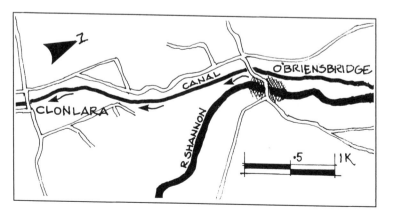

Walking time: 2 hours to Clonlara and back
Terrain: A comfortable, well-grazed grassy sward all the way, a little muddy in places in wet weather.
How to get there: O'Briensbridge, the starting and finishing point, is 4.8 km off the N7, 19 km east of Limerick.
Maps: OS Half-inch Sheets 17 and 18

O'Briensbridge is the site of an ancient fording place of the Shannon, whose broad and strongly flowing waters were first bridged here in the 16th century. A wide canal was constructed 1.5 km above the village to take off water from the Shannon to drive the turbines at Ardnacrusha, 8 km to the south-west. This walk follows the route of the Lough Derg Way along that canal from O'Briensbridge down to the next village, Clonlara.

Follow the main road westwards out of the village (take care where the road narrows) and after a few minutes a bridge over the canal is met. Cross an old cast-iron stile on the left just before the bridge signed 'The Lough Derg Way', and drop down to the grassy embankment lining the canal.

The broad embankment stretches ahead curving away into the distance, following the swift-moving waters of the diverted Shannon which is surprisingly broad and lined on the far side with a coniferous plantation.

Apart from the great construction works at Parteen upstream and Ardnacrusha downstream, it is clear that the work involved in the construction of this canalised river alone was prodigious. At the height of the work on the Shannon Scheme some 5,000 men were employed by the German contractors, Siemens-Schuckert, and newspapers of the time described the construction as the eighth wonder of the world.

After a few minutes the original Shannon comes into view to the left, at a considerably lower level than the canal, and looking back, the nine arches of the stone bridge at O'Briensbridge, built early in the 18th century. Soon after, a masonry stile is crossed; a sign here says 'Private Property — It is dangerous to trespass and the public do so at their own risk. It is unsafe to bathe in this area.' The Cospóir-approved Lough Derg Way, however, follows this same route, and I found no threats to health or safety that would not exist on any canal bank.

Further on, the riverine nature of the canal seems to assert itself, particularly on the far side, where the banks wander into reed-filled inlets which were occupied by small flocks of black-and-white tufted ducks when I passed here.

From the comparative height of the embankment there are extensive views across the green and fertile Shannon basin to the rolling Slieve Felim mountains. The Shannon river is no longer in sight, having taken a sharp turn south after O'Brien's bridge to flow to the Doonass Falls. During the construction work the German technicians had a canteen at Doonass House, not realising that a wine licence was required; a group of them were prosecuted under the Shebeening Acts and 1,400 bottles of wine were seized!

The canal sweeps through long meanders, giving at each clear views into the distance of the walk ahead. After about 30 minutes the silhouette of a slender modern bridge comes into view. To the left of it the pinnacles of a church tower rise, signalling the location of your destination, the hamlet of Clonlara.

In a deep declivity to the left, and out of view, a much older and now disused canal runs; the sound of its waters passing over a lock can be heard from near a ruined lock-keeper's cottage. This is the original Shannon navigation canal, built in the 1790s.

Sweeping around to the left, the embankment passes under a long net strung across the canal between two gantries, and then narrows to pass under the slender concrete bridge seen earlier. Climb a stile on to the bridge; the village of Clonlara is a couple of hundred metres to the left. There are two pubs there to offer refreshment before your return to O'Briensbridge, the Boree Log and the picturesque thatched premises of M. Stritch, whose sign proclaims it was established in 1786.

♦ WALK 58: THE SHANNON–ERNE WATERWAY, LEITRIM VILLAGE, CO. LEITRIM ♦

Work began on the link between the Shannon and Lough Erne in 1846, and by the late 1850s the canal system was in use. It was never a success, however, and was practically disused as early as the 1880s. In recent years it has been refurbished with the aid of regional development funding, and when I walked there I found it bustling with activity, with frequent cruisers passing north and south. Those used to the old canals will find the traffic lights and smart card-operated locks a culture shock! There are, at time of writing, no proper towpaths to be found, contrary to the indications on the official navigational guide maps. The banks are passable, however, if rough in places, the only problems being 'tributary' streams entering the canal that have no bridges. Always check with the local Office of Public Works personnel, whom I found very helpful and informative, before setting out on a stretch.

The walk described is a sample of what to expect on the newly refurbished system, following the canal from near Leitrim village to Lough Scur, and looping around Keshcarrigan Hill and the burial place of Finn Mac Cumhaill before returning to the start.

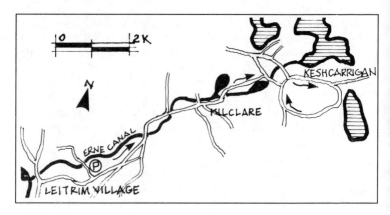

Walking time: 5½ hours there and back
Terrain: Canal banks, sometimes rough, and quiet tarmac roads.
How to get there: Leitrim village is on the T54, 7 km north of Carrick-on-Shannon. Approaching from the south, before crossing the bridge into the village, take the turn to the right, and after 500 m a turn to the left which will bring you down to Lock 16.
Maps: OS Half-inch Sheet 7, and the *Navigational Guide to the Shannon–Erne Waterway*

Leave Lock 16 and head north-eastwards as the beautifully paved area around the lock gives way to a rough and grassy canal bank. Although towpaths were constructed along some stretches of this canal originally, they were regarded as wasteful expenditure because much of the canal was through lakes where horse towage was impossible, and by the 1850s much of the traffic on the Shannon was steam powered. Ahead to the left is a flat-topped limestone hill, surmounted by a mound with a cross on it. The name of the hill is Sheemore, suggesting that the mound was once thought of as a fairy hill, until Christianity came along and borrowed the magic!

I cannot remember where I have seen such a range of grasses as I found here beside the canal; timothy grass, holy grass, slender foxtail and quaking grass were all represented, in addition to a variety of bamboo grass. In autumn they must attract a great richness of seed-eating birds.

Ten minutes after setting out, bridge number 2 is reached; it is such a pity that the names of these old bridges seem to have been forgotten and have been replaced unimaginatively by numbers. Go through a gate on to the road, cross the bridge to the far side and make your way down to Lock 15. With all the automation involved in the system, and in spite of the condition of the canal banks, I still found it possible easily to overtake cruisers going in the same direction along this stretch, which gave a little glow of satisfaction!

After the 15th lock the canal bank broadens into a pleasant meadow of tall grasses and wildflowers, and then narrows again before reaching bridge number 3. Beyond the bridge the ground is rougher, consisting of cattle-trampled soil that hardens in dry weather to test your ankles. There were lots of rabbits along here when I passed, scurrying in all directions for cover at my approach. There are also some drainage channels to be negotiated, but I found them reasonably dry and easy to cross.

Just before bridge number 4 there is a particularly rough section, which means having to turn a short distance 'inland' to cross a drainage channel, and it is a relief to reach the bridge and lock beyond. A favourable aspect of this section of the Shannon–Erne is the frequency of bridges and locks, which ensures that even the rough sections are limited, and there is always the possibility of escape!

Rounding a bend after lock number 13 the blue-grey whaleback shape of Slieve Anierin (the Iron Mountain) comes into view ahead. Tradition has it that the men of Finn Mac Cumhaill's Fianna lie spellbound in an enchanted cave on the mountain, awaiting a call to rise up and rescue Ireland from tyranny.

After bridge number 6 the clover-carpeted canal bank bends around to the right and passes by Lock 11 to reach a welcome sight on the far side, Lynch's pub and shop at the hamlet of Kilclare. Cross the bridge and continue on the southern side of the canal; the canal bank becomes difficult after Kilclare, so after Lock 9 continue along the tarmac and cross bridge number 8.

On the left at Bridge 8 is an extensive swamp, the centre of which is a reed-filled lake called Lough Conway; beyond this, the canal had to be cut from a low, limestone hill, and the extent of the work involved can be seen a few minutes later at narrow bridge number 11. Continue along the tarmac road to Drumaleague Lough, a reed-fringed lake through which the navigation passes, and turn left to cross over the canal again. Here the canal cuts through another hill; sheer walls of limestone rise up from the water, and it is easy to imagine why as many as 7,000 men were employed initially in the canal's construction.

At this stage the canal-side section of our walk is over; the return to the lock above Leitrim village will take about 2 hours. For the more energetic, however, I include an additional loop that takes you up and around Keshcarrigan Hill, from where there are great views all round, before returning, adding a further 1½ hours' walking time.

Follow the road over the bridge and take the first turn left. Pass the junction to the left for Roscarban bridge, and within minutes Scur Lough comes into view down to the left. It is an extensive and beautiful stretch of water scattered with islands with thought-provoking names such as Whiskey Island and Prison Island. A gate from a lay-by on the road gives access to a collapsed portal dolmen called locally Diarmuid and Grainne's Bed, one of the many to be found about the country.

Continue along the road, keeping right; the main road will bring you if you wish into the village of Keshcarrigan where there is a hostel, a shop, pubs and a craft centre. The road narrows and climbs past a quarry overlooking Keshcarrigan Lough, yet another of the fine lakes in this area. Continue to keep right, passing a holy well, and just after a flat-roofed house on the left, a prominent burial cairn can be seen on the summit ahead. A stile gives access to the cairn, which is said to be the burial place of the legendary champion Finn Mac Cumhaill. From the cairn the view is of a landscape of rounded drumlins patterned with rectangular hedged fields, interspersed with small silver lakes.

Follow the road as it goes steeply downhill and keep right at the next two junctions; at the third junction turn left to return to the canal.

A BRIEF BIBLIOGRAPHY

Bence-Jones, Mark, *A Guide to Irish Country Houses*, Constable, 1988.

Corcoran, Kevin, *West Cork Walks*, O'Brien, 1991.

Delany, Ruth, *Ireland's Inland Waterways*, Appletree, 1992.

Ellison, Cyril, *The Waters of the Boyne and Blackwater*, Blackwater, 1983.

Evans, Estyn, *Mourne Country*, Dundalgan, 1989.

Feehan, John, *The Landscape of Slieve Bloom*, Blackwater, 1979.

Fewer, Michael, *By Cliff and Shore*, Anna Livia, 1992.

Fewer, Michael, *The Way-marked Trails of Ireland*, Gill & Macmillan, 1996.

Flanagan, Laurence, *A Dictionary of Irish Archaeology*, Gill & Macmillan, 1992.

Guide to the Grand Canal, Inland Waterways Association of Ireland, 1992.

Guide to the Royal Canal, Office of Public Works, 1994.

Harbison, Peter, ed., *The Shell Guide to Ireland*, Gill & Macmillan, 1989.

Haughton Crowe, W., *The Ring of Mourne*, Dundalgan, 1969.

Herman, David, *Hillwalker's Connemara & Mayo*, Shanksmare, 1996.

Joyce, P. W., *Irish Names of Places*, M. H. Gill, 1895.

Joyce, W. St J., *The Neighbourhood of Dublin*, M. H. Gill, 1921.

Moriarty, Christopher, *Down the Dodder*, Wolfhound, 1991.

O'Sullivan, T. F., *Goodly Barrow*, Ward River, 1983.

Praeger, Robert Lloyd, *The Way That I Went*, Figgis, 1980.

Trench, C. E. F., *Slane Town Trail and Newgrange*, An Taisce, 1995.